THE LENTEN SPRING
Readings for Great Lent

THOMAS HOPKO

THE LENTEN SPRING

Readings for Great Lent

ST. VLADIMIR'S SEMINARY PRESS
CRESTWOOD, NEW YORK 10707
1983

Library of Congress Cataloging in Publication Data

Hopko, Thomas.
    The lenten spring.

    Bibliography: p.
    1. Lent—Prayer-books and devotions—English.
I. Title.
BX383.H66   1983   242'.34   83-4278
ISBN 0-88141-014-4

PRINTED IN THE UNITED STATES OF AMERICA
BY
ATHENS PRINTING COMPANY
NEW YORK, NY

In gratitude to the people of

St. John's Church, Warren, Ohio
St. Gregory's Church, Wappingers Falls, N.Y.
St. Nicholas' Church, Jamaica Estates, N.Y.

Contents

1

The Lenten Spring Shines Forth

The lenten spring shines forth,
the flower of repentance!
Let us cleanse ourselves from all evil,
crying out to the Giver of Light:
"Glory to You, O Lover of man!"[1]

The Church welcomes the lenten spring with a spirit of exultation. She greets the time of repentance with the expectancy and enthusiasm of a child entering into a new and exciting experience. The tone of the church services is one of brightness and light. The words are a clarion call to a spiritual contest, the invitation to a spiritual adventure, the summons to a spiritual feat. There is nothing gloomy here, nothing dark or remorseful, masochistic or morbid, anxious or hysterical, pietistic or sentimental.

The lenten spirit in the Church is one of splendor and delight. It breathes with the exhilaration of those girding up to "fight the good fight" for the One who loves them and has given Himself to them for the sake of their salvation.

The grace of abstinence has shone forth,
banishing the darkness of demons.
The power of the Fast disciplines our minds.
Lent brings the cure to our crippling worldliness.

[1]Cheesefare Wednesday vespers. The expression "Lover of man" (*Philanthropos*) appears many times in the verses and hymns here quoted. It may also be rendered as "Friend of man." Man, here, obviously means all human beings.

In the Orthodox Church there is a pre-lenten period of liturgical prepara-

Daniel and the Children in Babylon were strengthened
    by fasting;
one stopped the mouths of lions,
while the others extinguished the flames of the furnace.
As You saved them, save us also, O Christ our God,
for You are the Lover of man.[2]

Before the time of the saving Cross
sin ruled over all the earth,
impiety prevailed,
people revelled in the pleasures of the flesh.
But since the mystery of the Cross was accomplished
and the torture of demons was destroyed by the
    knowledge of God,
the heavenly life of virtue has reigned upon the earth.
Therefore the Fast is honored!
Abstinence shines in splendor!
Prayer is strengthened!
The lenten season testifies to these things,
given to us by our God, the crucified Christ,
for the salvation of our souls.[3]

How sad that people misunderstand the significance of
the lenten spring. How distressing that so many take this
time "given by our God, the crucified Christ" as a season for
sentimental devotions, anxious introspections and pietistic
pseudo-sufferings "together with Jesus." And how depressing
that others naturalize and rationalize the time with tepid
explanations about the psychosomatic benefits of abstinence
with arguments drawn from one or another therapeutic theory.

tion for the Fast, each week with its own theme. First there is the week of
the Publican and the Pharisee, then the Prodigal Son, then the week called
Meatfare, with the theme of the Final Judgment, finally the week of Cheesefare, with the double theme of the expulsion of Adam and Eve from Paradise
and the present need for forgiveness. The Sunday before the Monday on
which Great Lent begins is called both Cheesefare Sunday and Forgiveness
Sunday, because the faithful enter the lenten season forgiving one another.
The Meatfare and Cheesefare weeks traditionally end the eating of meat and
dairy products respectively until Easter.
    [2]Cheesefare Thursday matins.
    [3]Cheesefare Friday matins.

And how totally tragic that still others reject the whole affair, often with good reason because of its distortion, as a barbarous hangover from the dark ages to be radically rejected in these liberated and enlightened modern times.

The lenten spring is welcomed by Christians in the Church not as the time for self-inflicted agony or self-improving therapy. It is greeted as the sanctified season consecrated to the correction, purification and enlightenment of the total person through the fulfillment of the commandments of the crucified God. It is received as the time for battling with evil spirits and blossoming with the fruit of the Holy Spirit: love, joy, peace, patience, kindness, goodness, faithfulness, gentleness, self-control (Gal. 5:22). It is accepted as "the great and saving forty days" set apart for complete and total dedication to the things of God. It is the "tithe of the year" which tells us that all times and seasons belong to the Lord who has created and redeemed the world.[4]

The door of divine repentance has been opened.
Let us enter with fervor, having cleansed our bodies,
observing abstinence from foods and passions in
    obedience to Christ
who has called the whole world to His heavenly kingdom,
offering to the Master of all this tithe of the year,
that we may look with love upon His Holy Resurrection.[5]

The grace of the Lord has shone forth,
the grace which illumines our souls.
This is the acceptable time;
the time of repentance is here.
Let us put aside the works of darkness;
let us put on the armor of light,
that passing through Lent as through a great sea
we may reach the third-day Resurrection of our Lord
    Jesus Christ,
the Savior of our souls.[6]

[4]On the lenten season being a "tithe" of the year, see Dorotheos of Gaza, *On the Holy Lenten Fast*.
[5]Cheesefare Monday matins.
[6]Forgiveness Sunday vespers.

2

Let Us Begin with Joy

Joy is at the heart of everything in the Christian life, and Great Lent is no exception. The hymns and verses of the church services call Christians to begin with rejoicing.

Let us enter the Fast with joy, O faithful.
Let us not be sad.
Let us cleanse our faces with the waters of dispassion,
blessing and exalting Christ forever.[1]

Let us begin the Fast with joy.
Let us give ourselves to spiritual efforts.
Let us cleanse our souls.
Let us cleanse our flesh.
Let us fast from passions as we fast from foods,
taking pleasure in the good works of the Spirit
and accomplishing them in love
that we all may be made worthy to see the passion of
    Christ our God
and His Holy Pascha,
rejoicing with spiritual joy.[2]

Jesus commands all those who fast to be joyful. He condemns sadness and grief, especially the outward appearance of fasting before men. He orders His people to hide their sorrow and to cover their sadness over sin. He directs them to hide

[1]First Friday matins.

[2]Forgiveness Sunday vespers. "Pascha" is the Church's word for Easter, the feast of Christ's Resurrection. It literally means "Passover."

their acts of penitence, to keep their mortifications secret, to appear shining and bright to the world.

> And when you fast, do not look dismal, like the hypo-
> crites, for they disfigure their faces that their fasting
> may be seen by men. Truly, I say to you, they have
> their reward. But when you fast, anoint your head and
> wash your face, that your fasting may not be seen by
> men but by your Father who is in secret; and your
> Father who sees in secret will reward you. (Mt.
> 6:16-18)

Sadness for Christians is a sin to be repented of—not a virtue to be cultivated. Blessed mourning over the tragedies of this fallen world is possible. Those who mourn for this cause are promised comfort by the Lord. And godly grief over sins for the sake of leading us to conversion and repentance is possible. The apostle Paul refers to this in his second letter to the Corinthians.

> . . . I rejoice, not because you were grieved, but because
> you were grieved into repenting; for you felt a godly
> grief, so that you suffered no loss through us. For
> godly grief produces a repentance that leads to salva-
> tion and brings no regret, but worldly grief produces
> death. (2 Cor. 7:9-10)

In the lenten season the Christian struggles to put aside all "worldly grief" and to embrace the "godly grief" which St. John Climacus calls the "blessed joy-grief of holy compunc-tion," which inspires "spiritual laughter in the soul," since "God does not ask or desire that a person should mourn from sorrow of heart, but rather that out of love for Him he should rejoice with spiritual joy."[3]

As I ponder the true nature of compunction, I find

[3] St. John Climacus, *The Ladder of Divine Ascent*, step 7. St. John died in the seventh century. His memory is kept liturgically on the Fourth Sunday of Lent.

myself amazed by the way in which inward joy and
gladness mingle with what we call mourning and grief,
like honey in a comb. There must be a lesson here and
it surely is that compunction is properly a gift from
God, so that there is real pleasure in the soul, since
God secretly brings consolation to those who in their
hearts are repenting.[4]

These words of one of the severest of saints recall the
teachings of St. John Cassian, who lived about three hundred
years earlier.

The only form of dejection we should cultivate is the
sorrow which goes with repentance for sin and is
accompanied by hope in God. It was of this form of
dejection that the apostle said: "Godly sorrow produces a repentance that leads to salvation and brings
no regret" (2 Cor. 7:10). This "godly sorrow" nour-
ishes the soul through the hope engendered by repentance, and it is mingled with joy. That is why it makes
us obedient and eager for every good work: accessible,
humble, gentle, forbearing and patient in enduring all
the suffering or tribulation God may send us. Possession of these qualities shows that a person enjoys the
fruits of the Holy Spirit: love, joy, peace, long-
suffering, goodness, faith, self-control (see Gal. 5:22).
But from the other kind of dejection we come to know
the fruits of the evil spirit: listlessness, impatience,
anger, hatred, contentiousness, despair, sluggishness in
prayer. So we should shun this second form of dejection as we would unchastity, avarice, anger and the
rest of the passions. It can be healed by prayer, hope
in God, meditation on holy scripture and by living
with godly people.[5]

These lessons from the saints are the teaching of the Church
herself in her services for the lenten spring. Repentance and

---

[4]Ibid.
[5]St. John Cassian, *On the Eight Vices.*

joy, compunction and consolation, godly grief and spiritual rejoicing are joined together in perfect union in the person who fights for the Lord.

> Receive Lent with gladness, O people!
> The beginning of spiritual warfare arrives.
> Forsake the indulgences of your flesh
> that the gifts of the Spirit may abound in you.
> Embrace your share of suffering, O soldiers of Christ!
> Prove yourselves to be children of God!
> The Holy Spirit will take up His abode in you
> and your souls will be filled with His light.[6]

> "Only one day," He said,
> "is the life of those on earth."
> For those who make the effort in love
> there are forty days of the Fast
> for us to accomplish with joy.[7]

[6]Cheesefare Tuesday matins.
[7]First Monday matins.

3

Sanctify a Fast, Gather the People

Blow the trumpet in Zion; sanctify a fast;
call a solemn assembly; gather the people.
Sanctify the congregation; assemble the elders;
gather the children, even nursing infants.
Let the bridegroom leave his room, and the bride
    her chamber.
Between the vestibule and the altar
let the priests, the ministers of the Lord, weep
and say, "Spare Thy people, O Lord,
and make not Thy heritage a reproach, a byword
    among the nations.
Why should they say among the peoples,
'Where is their God?' " (Joel 2:15-17)

The lenten season is inaugurated in the Church with the
words of the prophet Joel. The message is proclaimed in the
midst of the congregation: "Sanctify a fast, call a solemn
assembly. Gather the elders and all the inhabitants of the
land to the house of the Lord your God; and cry to the Lord"
(Joel 1:14).

The fast is proclaimed because the people have sinned.
They have lost the protection of God because of their offenses.
They have been unfaithful. They have gone after false gods.
They have served the creature rather than the Creator who is
God over all. Their minds have grown dark. Their hearts
have become hard. Their necks have grown stiff. Their bodies
have been defiled. They have lost the joy and gladness that
comes from communion with the Lord. They have all gone

16

astray, every one to his own way. And the power of wicked-ness has overcome them. So every one of them, from the least to the greatest must return to the Lord. It is a corporate action, a total effort from which no one is excluded. It is an act of the Church herself.

"Yet even now," says the Lord, "return to Me with
    all your heart,
with fasting, with weeping, and with mourning;
and rend your hearts and not your garments."
Return to the Lord, your God, for He is gracious
    and merciful,
slow to anger, and abounding in steadfast love,
and repents of evil. (Joel 2:12-13)

These words of the prophet concerning the goodness and mercy of the Lord are familiar to those who know the scrip-tures and participate in the services of the Church. They are first recorded in the Law of Moses, revealed on Sinai itself.[1] They are repeated by all the prophets. They are sung over and again in the psalms at the liturgical gatherings of God's people.

The Lord is merciful and gracious,
slow to anger and abounding in steadfast love.
He will not always chide,
nor will He keep His anger for ever.
He does not deal with us according to our sins,
nor requite us according to our iniquities.
For as the heavens are high above the earth,
so great is His steadfast love toward those who fear Him.
As far as the east is from the west,
so far does He remove our transgressions from us.
As a father pities his children,
so the Lord pities those who fear Him.
For He knows our frame; He remembers that we are
    dust.[2] (Ps. 103:8-14)

[1]Ex. 34:6.
[2]One of the six matinal psalms in the Orthodox Church.

It is before the merciful and gracious Lord that all are called
to mourn and weep for their sins. It is before the Lord who
abounds with steadfast love that we are to "rend our hearts,"
and not simply our garments. It is to Him, whose steadfast
love is better than life, that we are commanded to return.[3]
He is the Father in Christ's parable of the prodigal son. He
stands waiting in the opened door of His house with robes
in His hands, music playing, the table abundantly laid. He
runs to meet His children who return home. He takes them
in His arms and returns them to the joy and gladness of their
proper inheritance. He pours out upon them all the riches of
His fatherly goodness.

> The Lord answered and said to His people,
> "Behold, I am sending to you grain, wine and oil,
>   and you will be satisfied;
>   I will no more make you
>   a reproach among the nations. . . .
>
> "Fear not, O land; be glad and rejoice,
>   for the Lord has done great things! . . .
>
> "Be glad, O sons of Zion,
>   and rejoice in the Lord, your God; . . .
>
> "You shall eat in plenty and be satisfied,
>   and praise the name of the Lord your God,
>   who has dealt wondrously with you."
>   (Joel 2:19-26)

The message of Joel ends, as that of all of God's prophets,
with words of restoration and blessing. It is this that we
seek in the lenten spring.

> Rich and fertile was the earth allotted to us,
> but all we planted were the seeds of sin.
> We reaped the harvest of evil with the sickle of laziness.

[3]See Ps. 63:3.

We failed to place our evil fruits on the threshing
    floor of contrition.
So now we beg You, O Lord, the Master of the harvest:
May Your Love become like the wind that blows
    away the straw of our worthless deeds,
and make us like the precious wheat to be stored in
    heaven,
and save us all![4]

[4]Sunday of the Prodigal Son vespers.

4

Return to the Father

From beginning to end the lenten services of the Church call us to return to God our Father. The theme of the parable of the prodigal son runs through the entire season.[1] We have wasted what our good God has given us. We have ruined our lives and our world. We have polluted the air, the water and the earth. The birds and the fish, the plants and the animals, grieve because of our wickedness. We have corrupted our bodies and minds. We have abandoned communion with God and the joy of His dwelling. We have gone off on our own, following our own ideas, enacting our own plans. And the result is that we are away from our true home, lost in a far country, living among swine. Through our reckless wasting of the gifts given by God we have stripped ourselves of our original glory, wisdom, beauty and strength: we have lost our divine legacy as children of God. And the whole cosmos suffers with us in our affliction.

> What great blessings have I forsaken, wretch that I am?
> From what kingdom have I miserably fallen?
> I have squandered the riches which were given to me.
> I have transgressed the commandments.
> Woe to me when I shall be condemned to eternal fire!
> Cry out to Christ, O my soul, before the end draws near:
> "Receive me as the prodigal, O God, and have mercy
>   on me."[2]

[1]The third week before Lent begins is liturgically dedicated to this parable. The theme continues through the entire season. See Lk. 15:11-32.
[2]Sunday of the Prodigal Son vespers.

I hid my face in shame, a wretched man.
I have squandered the riches my Father gave to me.
I went to live with senseless beasts.
I sought their food and hungered, for I had not enough
    to eat.
I will arise, I will return to my compassionate Father.
He will accept my tears as I fall before Him crying:
"In Your tender love for all people receive me as one
    of Your servants
and save me."[3]

People feel unhappy and they don't know why. They feel that something is wrong, but they can't put their finger on what. They feel uneasy in the world, confused and frustrated, alienated and estranged, and they can't explain it. They have everything and yet they want more. And when they get it, they are still left empty and dissatisfied. They want happiness and peace, and nothing seems to bring it. They want fulfillment, and it never seems to come. Everything is fine, and yet everything is wrong. In America this is almost a national disease. It is covered over by frantic activity and endless running around. It is buried in activities and events. It is drowned out by television programs and games. But when the movement stops and the dial is turned off and everything is quiet . . . then the dread sets in, and the meaninglessness of it all, and the boredom, and the fear. Why is this so? Because, the Church tells us, we are really not at home. We are in exile. We are alienated and estranged from our true country. We are not with God our Father in the land of the living. We are spiritually sick. And some of us are already dead.

Our hearts are made for God, St. Augustine has said, and we will be forever restless until we rest in Him. Our lives are made for God, and we will be unfulfilled and dissatisfied and frustrated until we go to Him. All of God's creatures, as Francis Thompson said in his poem *The Hound of Heaven,* are His "loyal betrayers." They do not satisfy His children

[3]Ibid.

and cannot bring them peace. He alone can do that, because
He alone is our home. And we are His.

The lenten season is the time for our conscious return to
our true home. It is the time set aside for us to come to ourselves and to get up and go to the divine reality to which we
truly belong.

> I have wasted in evil living the wealth which the
>   Father gave me,
> and I am now brought to emptiness,
> filled with shame and enslaved to fruitless thoughts.
> Therefore I cry to You, O Lover of man,
> "Take pity on me and save me!"[4]

> I am wasted with hunger, deprived of every blessing,
> an exile from Your presence.
> O Christ, supreme in loving kindness,
> take pity on me now as I return, and save me
> as I sing Your praises, O Lover of man.[5]

> Our purpose, O people, is to know the power of
>   God's goodness,
> for when the prodigal abandoned his sin
> he hastened to the refuge of his Father.
> That Good One embraced him and welcomed him.
> He killed the fatted calf and celebrated with heavenly
>   joy.
> Let us learn from this example to offer thanks to the
>   Father
> who loves all people,
> and to the Victim, the Lord Jesus Christ,
> the glorious Savior of our souls.[6]

---

[4]Sunday of the Prodigal Son matins.
[5]Ibid.
[6]Sunday of the Prodigal Son vespers. The expression "save our souls"
recurs often in the prayers and hymns. This does not mean that some
"spiritual part" of a person is valuable and the body, or the material generally,
is not. The word "soul" stands for the whole person and for life itself.

5

If I Forget You, O Jerusalem

The theme of man's exile from God, his estrangement from the true spiritual reality to which he belongs, is constantly repeated in the lenten services. We are not at home. We are not where we belong. We are alienated and estranged. We are in exile. This message is at the very heart of the biblical worldview. It is at the center of Christ's teaching, and that of His prophets, apostles, martyrs and saints of all ages. It is symbolized in many different ways in scriptural stories, parables and events. The lenten season makes use of them all. It is first proclaimed in the solemn chanting of Psalm 137 at the Sunday matins of the preparatory weeks before the beginning of Lent.

By the waters of Babylon,
    there we sat down and wept,
        when we remembered Zion.
On the willows there we hung up our lyres.
    For there our captors required of us songs,
        and our tormentors, mirth,
saying, "Sing us one of the songs of Zion!"

How shall we sing the Lord's song in a foreign land?
If I forget you, O Jerusalem,
    let my right hand wither!
Let my tongue cleave to the roof of my mouth,
    if I do not remember you,
        if I do not set Jerusalem above my highest joy!

Remember, O Lord, against the Edomites the day
    of Jerusalem,
    how they said, "Rase it, rase it! Down to its
        foundations!"
O daughter of Babylon, you devastator!
    Happy shall he be who requites you
    with what you have done to us!
    Happy shall he be who takes your little ones
        and dashes them against the rock!

Spiritually we are all by the waters of Babylon. Our true
home is Jerusalem; not a place on the map but a spiritual
reality. It is the true Jerusalem, the city of God, the Jerusalem
on high which, according to St. Paul, is "free, and she is our
mother" (Gal. 4:26).

But you have come to Mount Zion
and to the city of the living God, the heavenly Jerusalem,
and to innumerable angels in festal gathering,
and to the assembly of the first-born who are enrolled
    in heaven,
and to a judge who is God of all,
and to the spirits of just men made perfect,
and to Jesus, the mediator of a new covenant,
and to the sprinkled blood that speaks more graciously
    than the blood of Abel. . . .

Therefore let us be grateful for receiving a kingdom
    that cannot be shaken,
and thus let us offer to God acceptable worship,
with reverence and awe; for our God is a consuming
    fire. (Heb. 12:22-24, 28-29)

Christians await the "holy city, new Jerusalem, coming down
out of heaven from God, prepared as a bride adorned for
her husband," which is the true homeland of all human beings
(Rev. 21:2). They long to be taken up into that festal gathering where they will be inflamed with the fire of God. They
already live in it to the measure that they have discovered
their authentic humanity made in God's image and likeness

in Christ. Their sin is that they forget it in the present age and become comfortable in Babylon, pampering the passions of the flesh, which wage war against the soul to destroy it.[1]

To forget God is the cause of all sins. To be unmindful of Zion is the source of all sorrows. To settle down in this fallen world, which is not God's good creation but rather the Babylon which the wicked have made, is death to the soul.

> Do not love the world or the things in the world. If anyone loves the world, love for the Father is not in him. For all that is in the world, the lust of the flesh and the lust of the eyes and the pride of life, is not of the Father but is of the world. And the world passes away, and the lust of it; but he who does the will of God abides forever. (1 John 2:15-17)

The things of the world creep up on us to destroy us. We hardly notice it happening. Lust and pride and covetousness begin, little by little, to take over our lives. Their enslaving power always begins with little things. This is the spiritual meaning of the last line of Psalm 137, which scandalizes many people when they first hear it in literal terms. The "little ones" must be killed. The small temptations, the petty demons, the little sins, seemingly so innocent, insignificant and harmless, must be dashed upon the Rock of Christ. Otherwise they grow big and become strong and destroy the heedless and negligent with their lethal power.[2]

> Blinded by sensual pleasure,
> I bear within me a darkened soul,
> and the crafty enemy laughs when he sees me.
> Give me light, O Christ, and deliver me forever
>   from his malice.[3]

[1] See 1 Peter 2:11.

[2] In the prologue to his *Rule for Monasteries,* St. Benedict asks who shall dwell in the tent of the Lord and rest upon His holy mountain (Ps. 15). And he answers that it is he who, among other things, when tempted by the devil, "has laid hold of his [tempting] thoughts while they are still young and has dashed them against Christ."

[3] First Friday matins. The "enemy" referred to in the hymns is the devil.

6

Outside the Gates of Paradise

The basic symbol of man's loss of his original humanity and of his exile from God is the biblical story of the fall of Adam and Eve. Jokes about this sacred story abound. Comedians make fun of it in a sacrilegious manner. Commercials degrade it for money-making purposes. Even believers make light of it, with flippant remarks and pathetic attempts at humor. But the story is from God. And it is deadly serious. It tells of the most tragic event in human experience: the rebellion of the creature against the Creator and the transformation of the world as paradise with God into a garbage heap of dead men's bones. It describes this death-bound, demon-riddled, rat-racing world that we call human civilization, which is the result of the futile strivings of self-centered creatures.

Great Lent begins with the liturgical contemplation of the fall of Adam and Eve. The Sunday which marks the eve of the lenten season takes this story as its spiritual theme.

The Lord took a handful of dust from the earth.
He breathed into it and created me, a living man.
He made me lord and master of all things on earth.
Truly I enjoyed the life of the angels.
But Satan the deceiver, in the guise of a serpent,
    tempted me;
I ate the forbidden fruit and forfeited the glory of God.
Now I have been delivered to the earth through death.
O my compassionate Lord, call me back to Eden!

When the enemy tempted me I disobeyed Your command,
    O Lord.
I exchanged the glory of my immortal body for shame
    and nakedness.
Now I must wear garments of skins and fig leaves.
I am condemned to eat the bread of bitter hardship
    by the sweat of my brow.
The earth is cursed and brings forth thorns and
    husks for me.
O Lord, who took flesh from the Virgin in the
    fulness of time,
Call me back and restore me to Eden!

O paradise, garden of delight and beauty,
dwelling-place made perfect by God,
unending gladness and eternal joy,
the hope of the prophets and the home of the saints:
By the music of your rustling leaves
beseech the Creator of all to open to me the gates which
    my sins have closed,
that I may partake of the Tree of Life and grace
    which was given to me in the beginning.

Adam was exiled from paradise through disobedience.
He was driven from eternal bliss, deceived by the words
    of Eve.
He sat naked and weeping before the gates of paradise.
Let us hasten to enter the season of fasting;
let us carefully obey the Gospel commands,
that we may be made acceptable to Christ our God
and regain our home in Eden.

Adam sat before the gates of Eden.
bewailing his nakedness and crying out:
"Woe to me! I have listened to wicked deceit.
I have lost my glory and now am driven away.
Woe to me! My open-mindedness has left me naked
    and confused.
No longer will I enjoy your delights, O paradise.

No longer can I see my Lord, my God and Creator.
He formed me from dust and now to the dust I return.
I beg You, O compassionate Lord,
have mercy on me who have fallen!"[1]

In the Genesis story, filled with theological meaning and
spiritual significance, God does not say to His creatures: "Eat
of the tree and I will kill you." He says rather that "in the
day that you eat of it you shall die" (Gen. 2:17, RSV). The
tree is called the "tree of the knowledge of good and evil."
Knowledge in the Bible is not an abstract, intellectual thing.
It is not the product of thinking. It is the result of living
experience. The very word for knowledge in the Bible is the
word for the union of man and woman in marriage. When the
Bible says that "Abraham knew Sarah," it was not talking
about intellectual comprehension or analytical explanation.
It meant the experience of complete and total union. Eating
of the "tree of the knowledge of good and evil" means experiencing wickedness. It means committing sin. It means
tasting iniquity. It means doing an act which naturally and
organically devastates and destroys you.

Man is to fast from sin. He is to abstain from evil. He is
to refrain from drawing the destructive powers of wickedness into his system. He is to taste of life, to commune with
God, to be fed by righteousness, beauty and truth, to be
nourished by wisdom, goodness and love. Great Lent is the
time of year when we contemplate clearly what happens when
people do not do that. And it is the time when we make the
conscious effort to return to real life through the saving
action of Jesus Christ and the power of His Spirit through
communion with the "tree of life" planted and provided by
the God who loves us.

Adam ate the forbidden fruit and was driven from
     paradise.
He sat outside, weeping bitterly:
"Woe to me! What will become of me, the
     worthless man?

[1]Cheesefare Sunday vespers.

O holy paradise, planted for me by God and lost by
  the weakness of Eve,
grant that I may once again gaze on the flowers of
  your garden."
And the Savior said to him:
"I do not wish the death of My creation.
I desire that all should be saved and come to the
  knowledge of the truth.
For him who comes to me I shall never cast out."[2]

Adam was cast out from the delight of paradise
when he broke the commandment of the Master
  through uncontrolled desire.
His taking of food became bitter,
and he was condemned to work the earth from
  which he was taken;
he ate his bread in toil and sweat.
Therefore let us love abstinence, that we may enter
  through the gate
and not weep as he did outside of paradise.[3]

[2]Cheesefare Sunday vespers. The quotation is from 1 Tim. 2:4 and John
6:37.
[3]Cheesefare Sunday matins.

7

The Sin of Adam and Eve

All people inherit and imitate the sin of Adam and Eve.
We inherit sin just by being born in this world. This does
not mean that we are personally guilty for something which
our ancestors did.[1] It does mean, however, that we are sinful
from our very conception. We are already caught up in a
world alienated from God, broken and distorted, fragmented
and fallen. It means that we will inevitably die. It means that
our life is already "off the mark." ("Sin" means, literally,
"missing the mark.")

We imitate the sin of Adam and Eve by sinning ourselves.
We follow our first-parents by rebelling against God ourselves. We listen to the serpent, the spirit of evil, instead of
God. We do things in our own way. And we experience evil
for ourselves, by our own volition, and bring corruption to
our total being: mind, soul, heart and body. To the extent
that this wickedness is in us, we pass it on to those who come
after us, and they too become infected by evil from their very
conception.

> For I know my transgressions,
>   and my sin is ever before me.
> Against Thee, Thee only, have I sinned,
>   and done that which is evil in Thy sight,
> so that Thou art justified in Thy sentence,
>   and blameless in Thy judgment.

[1]Corporate guilt and repentance exist. For example, Christians must take
responsibility for and repent of the sins of the members of the Church as a
whole. But this does not mean that we are born with personal guilt for sins

30

Behold, I was brought forth in iniquity,
    and in sins did my mother conceive me.
    (Ps. 51:3-5, LXX)[2]

What exactly was the sin of Adam and Eve? By what
specific act did they betray their divine calling and distort
their nature made in the image and likeness of God? What
actually did they do? The scriptures are silent on this point.
There is no certain teaching. The eating of the fruit of the
tree of the knowledge of good and evil in the biblical story
signifies sinning in general. It stands for every kind of sin in
general and no specific sin in particular.

In every sin, whatever it is, there are always certain ele-
ments. It is these common characteristics of sin—all sin—that
the Genesis story discloses. There is, fundamentally, disobedience to God. There is the failure to listen to God and to
trust His words. There is always the temptation of the devil.
There is always pride and self-assertion. There is always and
in every case the failure to give thanks to God, to be grateful
for His gifts. And ultimately, as all of the Church's fathers
and saints insist, there is always self-love.

Life is a clash of loves. A person either loves God, and
so, with God, everyone and everything—for it is impossible
to love God and not to love all that God has created—or a
person loves himself. To love oneself does not mean to be
aware of one's value and worth before God. Such awareness
comes from receiving God's love and loving Him in return. To
love oneself sinfully, and as the cause of all sin, is to live
exclusively for oneself, to follow one's own thoughts and
ideas, to pursue one's own purposes and aims. It is to use
everyone and everything for one's own pleasure and self-
gratification. In this sense the love of self is the original sin.
It is at the heart of all wickedness. It is the very foundation
of all iniquity. It is the ultimate cause of death itself.

which we have not personally committed. The Orthodox doctrine of "original
sin" means that we are born *infected* by sin and its consequences. It does not
mean that we are born *guilty* for what others have done.

    [2]In the Greek translation of the Old Testament (the Septuagint, abbrevi-
ated LXX), the word "sin" in Ps. 51:5 is in the plural, as rendered here. It
is read this way in Orthodox church services.

The question asked by the Lord of Adam in his sin is the question that is asked of everyone at the beginning of Lent and throughout the season: Adam, where are you? (Gen. 3:9). Where is your heart? What do you live for? What do you love? For as Jesus, the true and perfect Adam, has said, "where your treasure is, there will your heart be also" (Mt. 6:21).

> You counted me worthy of honor in Eden, O Master,
> but, alas, in my wretchedness
> I was deceived by the envy of the devil
> and cast out from before Your Face.
>
> O ranks of angels,
> O beauty of paradise and all the glory of the garden:
> Weep for me, for I was led astray in my misery
> and rebelled against God.
>
> O blessed meadow, trees and flowers planted by God,
> O sweetness of paradise:
> Let your leaves, like eyes, shed tears on my behalf,
> for I am naked and a stranger to the glory of God.
>
> O precious paradise,
> I no longer see you nor delight in your splendor and joy,
> for I have angered my Creator
> and have been driven naked into the world.
>
> You have departed far from God through your
>   carelessness, O miserable soul.
> You have been deprived of the delight of paradise
>   and parted from the angels.
> You have been led down into corruption:
> How you are fallen![3]
>
> As once You gave paradise to Adam, O Word,
> now give me the joy of the fast

[3]Cheesefare Sunday matins.

that I may taste the sweetness of all Your command-
    ments, O God,
and never eat the forbidden fruit of sin.
With gladness I shall come to Your life-giving
    Passion on the Cross![4]

---

[4]First Tuesday vespers. In the Church's hymns, Jesus Christ is often
addressed as *Word*, or *Word of God*. This title comes from the Gospel
according to St. John.

8

Forgive, and You Will Be Forgiven

The Sunday before Lent begins, the day on which the Church liturgically remembers the fall of Adam and Eve, is called Cheesefare Sunday. This is because it is traditionally the last day of eating dairy products before the time of fasting. This day is also called Forgiveness Sunday since everyone must enter the lenten effort by forgiving and asking forgiveness of each other. In many churches, schools and monasteries this is done through a special "rite of forgiveness" following the evening vespers at which the Church formally inaugurates the lenten season. The significance of the act of giving and receiving forgiveness is obvious. God does not forgive us if we do not forgive each other. It is that simple.

> For if you forgive men their trespasses,
>   your heavenly Father also will forgive you;
> but if you do not forgive men their trespasses,
>   neither will your Father forgive your trespasses.
>   (Mt. 6:14-15)[1]

The Christian life is called the "imitation of God" by the fathers of the Orthodox Church. This conviction comes from the Bible, from the Old Testament, where the Lord through Moses says to His people: "consecrate yourselves therefore, and be holy, for I am holy" (Lev. 11:44)—a sentence quoted in the first letter of Peter in the New Testament:

> As obedient children, do not be conformed to the

[1]From the Gospel reading at the divine liturgy of Cheesefare (Forgiveness) Sunday.

passions of your former ignorance, but as He who
called you is holy, be holy yourselves in all your conduct; since it is written, "You shall be holy, for I
am holy." (1 Pet. 1:14-16)

Imitating the holiness of God is the task for human beings
set forth also by the apostle Paul. It is the specific task of
Christians.

Put off your old nature which belongs to your former
manner of life and is corrupt through deceitful lusts,
and be renewed in the spirit of your minds, and put on
the new nature, created after the likeness of God in true
righteousness and holiness. Therefore, putting away
falsehood, let every one speak the truth with his neighbor, for we are members one of another. . . . Let all
bitterness and wrath and anger and clamor and slander
be put away from you, with all malice, and be kind to
one another, tenderhearted, forgiving one another, as
God in Christ forgave you. Therefore be imitators of
God, as beloved children. (Eph. 4:22-25, 31-5:1)

The greatest possible "imitation of God" is to be forgiving.
God is the One who forgives. All of His love for man
(*philanthropia*) is love for sinners, "since all have sinned and
fall short of the glory of God" (Rom. 3:23).

None is righteous, no, not one;
    no one understands, no one seeks for God.
All have turned aside, together they have gone wrong;
    no one does good, not even one.
        (Rom. 3:10-12, quoting Ps. 14:3)

All humans are sinners. Anyone who claims not to be sinful
is a liar and makes God a liar as well:

If we say we have no sin, we deceive ourselves, and
the truth is not in us. If we confess our sins, He is
faithful and just, and will forgive our sins and cleanse

us from all unrighteousness. If we say we have not
sinned, we make Him a liar, and His word is not in us.
My little children, I am writing this to you so that you
may not sin; but if any one does sin, we have an advo-
cate with the Father, Jesus Christ the righteous; and
He is the expiation for our sins, and not for ours only
but also for the sins of the whole world. And by this
we may be sure that we know Him, if we keep His
commandments. He who says "I know Him" but dis-
obeys His commandments is a liar, and the truth is not
in him; but whoever keeps His word, in him truly love
for God is perfected. By this we may be sure that we
are in Him: he who says he abides in Him ought to
walk in the same way in which He walked. (1 Jn.
1:8-2:6)

Love between sinners is essentially expressed in forgiveness. There is no other way. It cannot be otherwise. Forgiveness is the singular expression of love in this fallen world. If,
therefore, we desire to be loved and forgiven by God—and
even more, if we know that as a matter of fact we are so loved
and forgiven—then we must love and forgive each other.
The lenten season exists for this purpose: to express the love
of God for one another through mutual forgiveness. This is
the teaching of Jesus Himself.

And whenever you stand praying, forgive, if you have
anything against any one; so that your Father also who
is in heaven may forgive you your trespasses. But if you
do not forgive, neither will your Father who is in
heaven forgive your trespasses. (Mk. 11:25-26)

Judge not, and you will not be judged; condemn not,
and you will not be condemned; forgive, and you will
be forgiven; give, and it will be given to you; good
measure, pressed down, shaken together, running over,
will be put into your lap. For the measure you give
will be the measure you get back. (Lk. 6:37-38)

In his novel *The Brothers Karamazov* the writer Fyodor
Dostoevsky puts the following teaching into the mouth of his
Elder Zossima: "Brothers, do not be afraid of men's sins.
Love man even in his sins, for that is the semblance of divine
love and is the highest love on earth." And later he adds, "At
some ideas you stand perplexed, especially at the sight of
men's sins, asking yourself whether to combat it by force or
by humble love. Always decide, 'I will combat it by humble
love.' If you make up your mind about that once and for all,
you may be able to conquer the whole world. Loving humility
is an awesome force, the strongest of all, and there is nothing
like it." It is this "awesome force" that we especially strive to
harness during the lenten spring. It is first of all the force of
forgiveness.

> O Master and Teacher of wisdom,
> Bestower of virtue,
> who teaches the thoughtless and protects the poor:
> Strengthen me and enlighten my heart.
> O Word of the Father,
> let me not restrain my mouth from crying to You:
> "Have mercy on me, a transgressor,
> O merciful Lord."[2]

²Kontakion of Forgiveness Sunday.

9

Open to Me the Doors of Repentance

After the reading of the Gospel at matins on each Lord's Day during the lenten season, the Church chants the following hymns of repentance:

Open to me the doors of repentance, O Life-giver,
for my spirit rises early to pray towards Your holy temple,
bearing the temple of my body all defiled.
But in Your compassion
purify me by the loving-kindness of Your mercy.

Lead me on the paths of salvation, O Mother of God,
for I have profaned my soul with shameful sins
and have wasted my life in laziness.
But by your intercessions
deliver me from all impurity.

When I think of the many evil things I have done,
wretch that I am,
I tremble at the fearful day of judgment;
but trusting in Your loving-kindness,
like David I cry out to You:
"Have mercy on me, O God, according to Your
    great mercy!"[1]

These hymns are related to the full recitation of Psalm 51, which is chanted year round at the church services—it

[1]The singing of these verses begins with the first pre-lenten Sunday, that of the Publican and the Pharisee, and continues throughout the entire season.

being, perhaps, the most-used psalm in the Orthodox liturgy.[2] It is the psalm attributed to David when he committed adultery and murder and then returned to God in repentance.

The New Testament begins with the preaching of repentance. St. John the Baptist begins his ministry with the message: "Repent, for the kingdom of heaven is at hand" (Mt. 3:2). Jesus Himself begins with these very same words (Mt. 4:17). He claims to come precisely to call sinners to repentance.

> Those who are well have no need of a physician, but those who are sick; I have not come to call the righteous, but sinners to repentance. (Lk. 5:31-32)

> Just so, I tell you, there will be more joy in heaven over one sinner who repents than over ninety-nine righteous persons who need no repentance. (Lk. 15:7)

> Just so, I tell you, there is joy before the angels of God over one sinner who repents. (Lk. 15:10)

These words of Jesus do not mean that there are people who have no need of repentance. According to the Lord, and to the entire scriptures of God, there is no person who is without sin and therefore without the need for repentance. The words of Jesus here are rather to emphasize how God loves every person, how He sends His Son for each lost soul, how Christ, the Good Shepherd, will leave the ninety-nine whom He already has in order to seek out and to save the one who is lost. Jesus' point is to insist on the value of every single person. He wants no one to be lost and dead. He wants every last one to be found alive with God.

We need to repent. This is the message. And repentance means change. It means a turning of one's mind and heart to God. It means the recognition of one's errors and faults and the firm desire to do something about it. It means violent

[2]Psalm 51 is regularly read at matins, third hour and compline. It is said by the celebrant of the Eucharist at the opening incensing of the church temple, and before the offering of the Gifts upon the altar.

action in the deepest and most hidden parts of the human spirit. It means brutal self-knowledge. It means open confession. It is an exacting affair involving one's total person and life. St. John Climacus, in his famous book *The Ladder of Divine Ascent,* defined repentance for Christians in this way:

Repentance is the renewal of baptism and is a contract with God for a fresh start in life. Repentance goes shopping for humility and is ever distrustful of bodily comfort. Repentance is critical awareness and a sure watch over oneself. Repentance is the daughter of hope and the refusal to despair. Repentance is reconciliation with the Lord by the performance of good deeds which are the opposites of the sins. It is the purification of conscience and the voluntary endurance of affliction. The repenting person deals out his own punishment, for repentance is the fierce persecution of the stomach and the flogging of the soul into intense awareness.[3]

May we all, through our abstinence, attain to this intense awareness of soul during the lenten spring.

Let us bring tears of repentance to the Lord, as
    did the publican.
Let us fall before Him as sinners before the feet
    of our Master,
for He desires the salvation of all people,
granting forgiveness to all who repent.
For He took human flesh for our sake
though He is God, co-eternal with the Father!

Let us all humble ourselves, O people,
groaning and lamenting and beating our conscience,
that on the Day of Judgment we may receive forgiveness
and be numbered with the righteous and faithful.
Let us pray to see the true peace of the age to come

[3]*The Ladder of Divine Ascent,* Step 5.

where there is no more sorrow or sighing,
In the glorious Eden fashioned by Christ,
for He is God, co-eternal with the Father![4]

---

[4]Kontakion and oikos of the Sunday of the Publican and the Pharisee.

10

More Than All Have I Sinned

During the first week of Lent the penitential Canon of St. Andrew of Crete is chanted each evening during compline.[1] It is an allegorical poem comparing the thoughts and deeds of the sinful soul with biblical characters and events. It is a cry for mercy and compassion which stresses the goodness of God and the forgiveness of all iniquities in Christ. Yet many of its lines strike the modern person as artificial and exaggerated. It makes claims which many people find impossible to affirm with conviction.

> More than all have I sinned;
> I alone have sinned against You.
> O God my Savior,
> have compassion upon me, Your creature.

> There has never been a sin, a deed, an evil act,
> which I have not cherished, O Savior.
> I have sinned in thoughts, words and deeds,
> and no one has sinned more than I.

> David was a forefather of the Lord, O my soul,
> yet he sinned doubly by committing both murder and
>   adultery.
> Your sickness, however, is even worse than his deeds
> because of your impulsive will.

[1]The canon is also chanted in its entirety at matins of Thursday of the Fifth Week.

David, though once compounding his sins
by first murdering a man and then stealing his wife,
was quick to repent of both.
You, however, O my soul, have done worse things than he,
yet you never repented of them before God.

I have sinned, Lord, I have sinned against You.
Be merciful to me
though there is no one whose sins I have not surpassed.[2]

Is it really right to say that I have sinned more than all others
and that there is no sin which I have never cherished? Does
it make sense to claim—in prayer before God no less—that
my sickness has surpassed that of David in his murder and
adultery? And that sinning more than all others, I have not
repented at all? Is this necessary? Is it true? Is it not rather
an unacceptable hangover in the Church of a spiritual style
that should be expunged from the life of God's people? Is
it not but one more example of that repulsive obsession with
sin, that pious fraud of inauthentic devotion, that disgusting
hyperbole of liturgical expression that tends more to turn
people off than to inspire them to authentic repentance and
genuine adoration and gratitude to God for His great mercy
poured out upon the world in the person of His Son?

Each person can answer these questions only for himself.
But there are certainly some, like St. Andrew of Crete and
those who have so identified with his supplications as to have
them become part of the Church's own prayer, who find sense
in such sayings and sing them with conviction. How can this
be? Something like the following seems to be the answer.

Every person stands alone before God. This is not to say
that we are isolated one from another in self-enclosed indi-
viduality. Just the opposite is in fact the scriptural claim:
"for we are members one of another" (Eph. 4:25). But we
are not in a spiritual contest with one another. And we are
not judged before God in comparison with each other. God's
judgment, as the saying goes, is not on a curve! Each person
is unique. Each person has his or her own calling and gifts.

[2]Canon of St. Andrew of Crete: Monday 2:3, 4:4, 7:5-6; Tuesday 3:2.

Each person has his or her own life to fulfil or to fail. Each
human being is personally judged according to God's righteous judgment, which applies strictly to that person alone.

Standing before God, one does not look at others. One
looks only at God. But in this mystical moment, this instant
of lucid insight concerning the meaning of all things in the
perspective of the unique soul before its Master, the spirit
can only cry out, in all integrity and conviction: I have sinned
as no other! In my unique personality, in the life which my
Maker has given to me, with what I have received from my
bountiful Lord, I have truly surpassed all in my sins! Each
person will feel this. Each soul will be convinced of it. No
rational analysis or logical deduction that it is patently absurd
will make any difference. A hundred people at the very same
service—and thousands, even millions, across time and space—
will be fully convinced that this is true for them alone. And it
is.

For each one, in the spiritual uniqueness of his or her
own life—especially in the Church of Christ where willful,
lustful thoughts are fornication and adultery, and hidden
movements of anger and judgment are torture and murder,
and the failure to share is thievery, and the failure to give is
covetous idolatry—will say with St. Paul with perfect conviction that "the saying is sure and worthy of full acceptance,
that Christ Jesus came into the world to save sinners, of whom
I am the first."[3] All Orthodox Christians claim this in the
prayer before receiving Holy Communion at all celebrations
of the Holy Eucharist. It is a spiritual fact which all affirm
and none deny who see themselves in the light of Christ
before the face of God in whose likeness they are formed
for life everlasting. Those of us for whom such prayers ring
untrue have yet, it seems, to authentically encounter the living
God.

Let us go quickly while there is still time,

[3]This is the literal translation of 1 Tim. 1:15, and is used liturgically in
the Orthodox Liturgy: "I believe, O Lord, and I confess that Thou art truly
the Christ, the Son of the Living God, who camest into the world to save
sinners, of whom I am first."

let us lament, let us be reconciled to God
    before the end comes.
For the judgment is fearful
at which we all shall stand naked.

The day is upon us;
judgment now is at the door.
Be vigilant, O my soul.
Princes and kings, rich people and poor are
    gathering together,
and each will be rewarded for what he has done.

Monks and bishops, slaves and masters, old and young,
each shall be examined in his proper place.
Widow and virgin shall be corrected,
and woe to all whose lives are sinful.

The judgment is without respect of persons.
No cunning defense or skill of speech can deceive the
    Judge.
False witnesses cannot pervert the sentencing,
for in Your sight, O God, every secret sin stands revealed.

I cry to You, O Lord:
"Have mercy, have mercy on me!
When You come with Your angels
to give due reward to each person for his deeds."

I have sinned as no other person before.
I have transgressed more than any other, O Lord.
Before the Day of Judgment comes,
be merciful to me, O Lover of Man.[4]

---

[4]Meatfare Sunday matins. The liturgical theme of this Sunday is the Last Judgment. The gospel reading at the Eucharist is Mt. 25:31-46. It is Orthodox doctrine that the grace of God and faith in Him are always expressed in deeds, and that it is by his deeds that a person is to be judged by the Lord. See Mt. 7:21; Rom. 2:6; Rev. 20:12, 22:12.

11

A Contrite and Humble Heart

When David the king sinned before God by murder and adultery, he repented with tears and was forgiven. Through the intercessions of Nathan the prophet he was reconciled with the Lord, being pardoned his transgressions. From the line of this penitent sinner comes Jesus the Messiah, whose reign on David's throne will have no end.

In his great psalm of repentance, David proclaims that God's steadfast love and mercy are greater than the iniquities of His creatures. God accepts a broken and humble heart before all sacrifices and offerings. To our contrition He replies with forgiveness.

Have mercy on me, O God,
   according to Thy steadfast love.
According to Thy abundant mercy,
   blot out my transgressions.
Wash me thoroughly from my iniquity,
   and cleanse me from my sin! (Ps. 51:1-2)

Fill me with joy and gladness;
   let the bones which Thou hast broken rejoice.
Hide Thy face from my sins,
   and blot out all my iniquities. (Ps. 51:8-9)

For Thou hast no delight in sacrifice;
   were I to give a burnt offering,
   Thou wouldst not be pleased.
The sacrifice acceptable to God is a broken spirit;

a broken and contrite heart, O God, Thou wilt
   not despise. (Ps. 51:16-17)

David humbled himself before God in his sin and was
forgiven. Others in the scriptures whose sins were not those
of David had the same reaction of contrition and compunction
before the face of God. Job was the most righteous man alive.
The Lord Himself said of him that "there is none like him
on the earth, a blameless and upright man, who fears God
and turns away from evil" (Job 2:3). God allowed Satan
to smite him, and even in his pain, while arguing and contending with the Lord, Job kept his perfect trust in God's
righteousness. Yet even Job fell down in contrition of heart
when he came to see the divine majesty with his own eyes.

I had heard of Thee by the hearing of the ear,
   but now my eye sees Thee;
therefore I despise myself,
   and repent in dust and ashes. (Job 42:5-6, RSV)[1]

The three young men in the book of Daniel refused to
worship the golden idol which King Nebuchadnezzar had
set up. They remain until today in the Church the very images
of faith in God and righteousness before Him.[2] In the exile
in Babylon, when they alone were faithful, they confessed
before the Lord that the offering of a contrite heart and a
humble spirit would forever be acceptable to the Most High
above all sacrificial offerings.

For we, O Lord, have become fewer than any nation,
   and are brought low this day in all the world
      because of our sins.
And at this time there is no prince, or prophet, or leader,
   no burnt offering, or sacrifice, or oblation, or incense,
      no place to make an offering before thee or to
         find mercy.

[1]The book of Job is read in the Church during Holy Week.
[2]The three young men in Babylon are hymned at each matinal canon in
the Orthodox Church. Their canticle sung in the fiery furnace is chanted at
the Lord's Day liturgy and at the paschal vigil.

Yet with contrite heart and a humble spirit may we
    be accepted,
        as though it were burnt offerings of rams and bulls,
            and with tens of thousands of fat lambs;
Such may our sacrifice be in thy sight this day,
        and may we wholly follow thee,
                for there is no shame for those who trust in thee.
And now with all our heart we follow thee,
        we fear thee and seek thy face.
                (Canticle of the Three Young Men, 15-19)

The apostle Peter could hardly look at Jesus without fall-
ing on his face or jumping into the sea. Sinful women threw
themselves at the Lord's feet, kissed them and washed them
with their tears. Even the demons cried out in Christ's presence—but without contrition—begging Him to leave and not
to torment them "before the time" (Mt. 8:29).

The lenten season is the time for direct confrontation with
God. It is the time for consciously presenting oneself before
the face of the Lord for judgment. There is nothing to be
offered, and no sacrifice is acceptable. There is only the broken
spirit and the contrite heart of repentance which God will
not despise.

Have mercy on me, O God, have mercy on me!

David once showed us the image of true repentance
in a psalm he wrote exposing all that he had done.
"Be merciful to me and cleanse me!" he wrote,
"For against You only have I sinned, the God of our
    fathers."

Have mercy on me, O God, have mercy on me!

I have distorted Your image, O Savior,
    and broken Your commandments.
The beauty of my soul has been spoiled,
    and its light extinguished by my sins.

But have pity on me and, in David's words,
  "Restore to me the joy of Your salvation."

Have mercy on me, O God, have mercy on me!

Return! Return! Uncover what is hidden!
Say to God who knows all things:
"You are my only Savior and know my terrible secrets.
Yet in David's words I cry to You:
'Be merciful to me, O God, according to Your steadfast
  love.' "

Have mercy on me, O God, have mercy on me!

O only Savior, do not require of me in my weakness
fruits which will show that I have changed my ways.
Grant rather that, finding contrition of heart and
  poverty in spirit,
I may offer these to You as a pleasing sacrifice.[3]

[3]Canon of St. Andrew of Crete: Monday 7:6; Thursday 7:3, 4; 9:4.

12

Planting the Word of God in the Heart

The grace of God is a divine power in our life. Without it we can do nothing. We are saved by grace, and grace alone. Yet the grace of God is given to us so that we might labor for the food which endures to eternal life (Jn. 6:27), that we might take up our cross and follow Christ (Mk. 8:34), that we might fight the good fight and endure to the end (1 Tim. 6:12, Mt. 24:13).

In his writings about the spiritual life, Bishop Ignatius Brianchaninov, a Russian elder of the last century, speaks about the relationship between God's grace and human labors. He uses the image of a farmer planting his fields.[1] The word of God must be planted in our hearts. The Spirit of God must be accepted into our souls. The grace of God must be received into our lives. In order to accept the grace of God's Word and Spirit within us, we must prepare the soil. It must be tilled and cultivated. It must be made loose and open, ready to receive what God showers upon it. If the soil is not ready, it cannot accept God's gracious actions. But if it is worked over and over, and the gracious Word is never received and implanted, it remains barren and fruitless. The spiritual teacher says that there are some who attempt to receive God's grace without the tilling. And there are others who till and till, but never accept the gracious Word within them. Both kinds of people, he warns, are subject to great evils:

The bread of heaven is the Word of God. The labor

[1]This image is inspired by Jesus' parable of the sower (Mk. 4, Mt. 13, Lk. 8). See also St. Paul's teaching in 1 Cor. 3.

50

of planting the Word of God in the heart requires such efforts or exertions that it is called a struggle. . . . Only a servant of Christ during his life on earth feeds on heavenly bread in the sweat of his brow by constantly struggling with the carnal mind, by constantly laboring at the cultivation of virtues. . . .

The man who would take it into his head to cultivate his land without using farm implements would have a heavy labor expenditure and would labor in vain. Just so, he who wants to acquire virtues without bodily discipline will labor in vain, will waste his time without reward and without return, will exhaust his spiritual and physical powers and will gain nothing.

Likewise a man who is always ploughing his land without ever seeding it will reap nothing. Just so, he who is incessantly occupied merely with bodily discipline will be unable to practice spiritual exercises, such as planting in his heart the commandments of the Gospel, which in due time bear spiritual fruits.

Bodily discipline is essential in order to make the ground of the heart fit to receive the spiritual seeds and to bear the spiritual fruits. To abandon or neglect it is to render the ground unfit for sowing and bearing fruit. Excess in this direction and putting one's trust in it is just as harmful, or even more so, than neglect of it.

Neglect of bodily discipline makes men like animals who give free rein and scope to their bodily passions. But excess makes men like devils and fosters the tendency to pride and the constant recurring of other passions in the soul.

Those who abandon bodily discipline become subject to gluttony, lust and anger in their crudest forms. Those who practice immoderate bodily discipline, use it indiscreetly, or put all their trust in it, seeing in it their own merit and worth in God's sight, fall into vainglory, self-opinion, presumption, pride, hardness and obduracy, contempt for their neighbors, detraction and condemnation of others, rancour, resentment, hate, blasphemy, schism, heresy, self-deception and diabolic delusion.

Let us give due value to bodily ascetic practices as instruments and means indispensable for acquiring the virtues, but let us beware of regarding these instruments as virtues in themselves so as not to fall into self-deception and deprive ourselves of spiritual progress through a wrong understanding of Christian activity.[2]

During the lenten spring we labor and toil through the proper use of bodily discipline and ascetic effort to "put away all filthiness and rank growth of wickedness and receive with meekness the implanted Word, which is able to save [our] souls" (Jas. 1:21).

Come, O faithful!
Let us glorify the fathers who lived the ascetic life in
     holiness.
Let us praise in one accord, with hymns inspired by God,
the servants of Christ who lived in fasting and abstinence,
showing us plainly the Gospel of Christ.
Let us also sing the praise of the holy and glorious women,
all those who bore God in their hearts.
Out of love for Him, let us follow their way of life,
that in the world to come we may receive the
     remission of our sins.[3]

---

[2]*The Arena*, ch. 35.
[3]Cheesefare Saturday matins. This day is liturgically dedicated to the saints who were "enlightened through ascetic efforts."

13

If We Confess Our Sins

It is not enough for us to know our sins and to hate them. We must also confess them before God and man. We must acknowledge them before heaven and earth. We must expose them to the whole of creation in order to be rid of them from within our secret hearts. Confession is part of the spiritual life. Indeed, it is part of life itself. There is no authentic existence for human beings without it. And there is certainly no authentic repentance.

> If we say we have no sin, we deceive ourselves, and the truth is not in us. If we confess our sins, He is faithful and just, and will forgive our sins and cleanse us from all unrighteousness. If we say we have not sinned, we make Him a liar, and His word is not in us. (1 Jn. 1:8-10)

Some say that there is no need to confess sins openly and publicly. They say that people can confess directly to God. Such an idea is total nonsense. Confession to God in secret is no confession at all. It is simply the acknowledgment before the Lord that we know what He knows! Confession by definition is open and public. If it is not, it is simply not confession.

When the people were repenting in preparation for Jesus at the preaching of John the Baptist, it is written that they were baptized "confessing their sins" (Mk. 1:5). This does not mean that they were telling God in the privacy of their hearts what He already knew. It means that they were pro-

claiming the evils that they had done for all to hear. And
when St. James commands Christians: "Confess your sins to
one another!" he is not advising them to be aware of their
transgressions in the secrecy of their souls. He is ordering
them to reveal their wickednesses to each other so that they
might be healed (Jas. 5:16).

If confession is by definition the open and public acknowledgment of sins, why then do the Orthodox confess privately
to their priests? It is not because the priests have some special
power which others do not have. To think this way is to be
highly mistaken, although many Christians have such an
understanding.[1] Priests have no power personally to forgive
sins. Only Jesus Christ has such power. But the pastors do
have the ministry of witnessing the confession and repentance
of God's people, and of officially sealing that confession and
repentance with the assurance of divine forgiveness through
the prayer of absolution.

The reason why people now confess to their pastors in
private is because of the weakness of the body of Christians
as a whole. Confession used to be public. It was done openly
in the presence of all of the members of the Church. Anyone willing to confess in this manner today is welcome to do
so. But it would most likely serve only to lead others into
temptation rather than to inspire prayerful compassion and
sympathetic collaboration in fulfilling the Lord's commandments. When confession is done to the priest alone, it should
be understood that it is to him as if it were to all. Or, to put
it another way, it is to all—God and man and the whole of
creation—in the priest's person, as the head of the church

[1]The fact that the priest is the sacramental presence in the Church of the
Lord Jesus Himself does not mean that he *personally* has Christ's power and
authority. The original prayer of absolution in the Orthodox Church does
not have the priest say, "I forgive and absolve you," just as the Orthodox
baptismal service does not have the priest say, "I baptize you." The first
person is not used. The power of forgiveness of sins (which in the scriptures
is, in any case, connected with baptism, and not confession) belongs to
Jesus alone. It is present in the Church because Jesus is present in the Church,
in all the members and particularly in the ordained priest who is His sacramental image in the church community. See Thomas Hopko, *If We Confess
Our Sins* (Department of Religious Education, Orthodox Church in America,
1975).

community and the sacramental presence within it of the Lord Jesus Himself.

Great Lent is a time for confession. All Christians should make their confession during this holy season. A person who fails to do so is hardly a Christian. He is certainly not Orthodox.

In his spiritual diary, Fr. Alexander Elchaninov gives advice about confession. Advice is also found in the writings of Fr. John of Kronstadt, and in such books as *Unseen Warfare* and *The Way of the Pilgrim.*[2] Christians should read writings of this sort to help them with their confession. Theophan the Recluse advised those preparing for confession to study the Sermon on the Mount (Mt. 5-7) and the first letter of John, together with 1 Corinthians 13 and Romans 12 to 14. These, and other sections of the scriptures, focus sharply on what is expected of Christians in their daily behavior.[3] Fr. Elchaninov writes that confession "springs from an awareness of what is holy, it means dying to sin and coming alive again to sanctity." It begins with "a searching of the heart." It moves to a sincere "contrition of the heart." It expresses itself in the "oral confession of sins," accomplished "with precision, without veiling the ugliness of sin by vague expressions." It is fulfilled in the resolution never to sin again, although realizing that we will fall because we are not God. It is sealed by our subsequent sufferings to remain steadfast in our struggle against sin. Such confession is at the heart of our spiritual efforts, especially during the lenten spring.

Behold, my child, Christ stands here invisibly and receives your confession. Wherefore be not ashamed nor afraid and conceal nothing from me, but tell without hesitation all things which you have done, and so you shall have pardon from our Lord Jesus Christ. Lo, His holy image is before us, and I am but a witness,

[2]Full bibliographical information for these and other books containing advice about confession may be found at the end of this book.

[3]Other scriptural passages recommended for use in preparing one's confession are Lk. 6:20-49; Gal. 5:13-6:10; Eph. 4:25-6:20; Phil. 2:1-18; Col. 3:1-4:6; 2 Tim. 2-3; and all of Jas.

bearing testimony before Him of the things which you
have to say. But if you shall conceal anything you shall
have the greater sin. Take heed, therefore, lest having
come to the physician, you depart unhealed.[4]

---

[4]Exhortation of the confessor to the penitent in the Rite of Confession
(Slavonic version).

14

Pray for Us, O You Saints!

Christians pray for each other and ask each other's prayers. In doing this they fulfill God's command to love one another, and actualize in a powerful way the fact that they are "members one of another" in Him (Eph. 4:25). "For just as the body is one and has many members, and all the members of the body, though many, are one body," says St. Paul, so it is with Christ. . . . Now you are the body of Christ and individually members of it" (1 Cor. 12:12, 27).

The body of Christ, which Christians compose as members of Christ in His Church, cannot be broken by anything. We can sever ourselves from the body because of our sins, but we cannot be separated from it by anything else.

The apostle Paul again says it most adequately: "For I am sure that neither death, nor life, nor angels, nor principalities, nor things present, nor things to come, nor powers, nor height, nor depth, nor anything else in all creation, will be able to separate us from the love of God in Christ Jesus our Lord" (Rom. 8:38-39).

The unity which Christians enjoy with each other in Christ, and with God and all people and the whole of creation in Him, is not destroyed by death. Those who "fall asleep in the Lord" are alive in Him. Being His holy servants on earth, they enter into eternal life with Him and His Father, by the abiding presence within them of His life-creating Spirit. They remain alive "in the heavens" with Jesus, appearing with Him in the presence of God to make intercessions on our behalf.[1]

[1] See Heb. 7:25; 9:24; 12:1-2, 18-29; Rev. 5:6-14; 6:9-11; 7:9-17.

If Christians ask each other's prayers while all are still on
earth, how much more should those who are still living in
the flesh beg the prayers of their brothers and sisters who
have already departed to be with Christ at the Father's right
hand? And especially of those whose sanctity has been revealed to the Church by the Lord Himself.

A particular feature of the lenten services is that the
repenting members of the Church still struggling on earth call
out in prayer to their brothers and sisters who are already
with the Lord, begging the assistance of their prayers and
intercessions. This is done in the Church throughout the entire liturgical year. It is especially done during Great Lent
when God's people contemplate their iniquities, call forth
their transgressions, expose their faults and proclaim their
separation from God because of their sins. Thus, at every
vespers on lenten weekdays, in place of the usual hymns for
the day, special troparia of intercession are sung, with prostrations outside the altar, before the closed gates of the
sanctuary.

Rejoice, O Virgin Theotokos, Mary full of grace!
    The Lord is with you.
Blessed are you among women, and blessed is the fruit
    of your womb,
for you have borne the Savior of our souls.

Glory to the Father and to the Son and to the Holy Spirit.

O Baptizer of Christ, remember us all,
that we may be delivered from our iniquities;
for to you is given grace to intercede for us.

Now and ever and unto ages of ages. Amen.

Intercede for us, O holy apostles and all the saints,
that we may be delivered from perils and sorrows,
for we have acquired you as fervent intercessors
    before the Savior.

Beneath your compassion we take refuge, O Theotokos.
Do not despise our supplications in adversity,
but deliver us from perils, O only pure and only
   blessed one.

At the great compline also, when the penitential Canon of St. Andrew of Crete is chanted, similar supplications are made, once more with prostrations outside the sanctuary, before the closed gates which symbolize man's separation from God and his exclusion from paradise.

O all-holy and sovereign Lady Theotokos, pray
   for us sinners.
O all the heavenly host of angels and archangels,
   pray for us sinners.
O holy John, prophet, forerunner, and baptist of our
   Lord Jesus Christ, pray for us sinners.
O holy, glorious apostles, prophets and martyrs, and
   all saints, pray for us sinners.
O all our reverend and God-fearing fathers, pastors,
   and ecumenical teachers, pray for us sinners.
O holy St. [patron of the church], pray for us sinners.
O invincible, ineffable, and divine power of the honorable
   and life-giving Cross, do not forsake us sinners.
O God, cleanse us sinners and have mercy on us!

"Therefore confess your sins to one another, and pray for one another, that you may be healed," says St. James. "The prayer of a righteous man has great power in its effects" (Jas. 5:16). These words from the scriptures are applicable to the righteous in heaven, the very content of whose being and life is to adore God and to intercede for us who are still struggling in the flesh for the salvation of our souls.

Come, O people!
Let us praise and glorify those who shone forth in the
   ascetic life.
Here on earth they lived in holiness and righteousness,
   and now are taken up into the joy of life eternal.

In holiness and virtue they ran the straight course
leading to the eternal blessings of the age to come.
Let us give them rightful honor
that through their intercessions we may obtain mercy,
        eternal joy and glory from God,
and escape unending punishment in the future life.

O choir of bishops and assembly of the righteous,
with the monastics and holy women who lived
        in godliness,
we pray that you will intercede with the Lord,
the only good and merciful One,
that He may have compassion upon us.
May we be delivered by your prayers, O saints,
from condemnation in the age to come,
and rejoice for all eternity in the blessedness of heaven,
crying out with ceaseless hymns of praise to the Giver
        of Life![2]

---

[2]Cheesefare Saturday matins. This day is liturgically dedicated to those who have been enlightened through ascetic efforts.

15

Lord, Have Mercy

The most repeated prayer in Orthodox liturgical worship is *Kyrie eleison:* Lord, have mercy. It is sung again and again: once, three times, twelve, forty, seventy, a hundred. In the evening and the morning, at noonday and at midnight, it is always the same: Again and again let us pray to the Lord. Lord, have mercy!

What is the meaning of this constant prayer for mercy? Is it, once again, an indication of the Church's obsession with sin, a penitential cry to the fearful Judge for pardon and pity? Some people think so. One person wrote that the Orthodox liturgy became filled with "Lord, have mercy" under the influence of the monks who, as professed penitents, spend every waking hour begging God not to condemn them for their transgressions!

While it is true that all people have sinned and require the forgiveness of God, the prayer "Lord, have mercy" is hardly a simple plea for pardon and acquittal. It is much more than that. In its literal meaning, it is not even that at all. The very fact that the Church sings "Lord, have mercy" as a response to all of her prayers and petitions, including those for peace, health and good weather, as well as those of praise and thanksgiving, should demonstrate this quite clearly. The fact that the Church continues to sing "Lord, have mercy" on the most joyous and gracious of occasions, like after Holy Communion and on Easter night, should also be considered.

It is the word "mercy" that leads to a wrong understanding of the *Kyrie eleison.* We tend today to think of mercy almost exclusively in terms of justice. The opposite of being

justly judged, and therefore condemned, is to receive mercy.
So the "Lord, have mercy" gets interpreted as "Lord, grant
us pardon!" Or, "Lord, let us off!" In the scriptures and
tradition, however, mercy is not primarily the antonym of
justice. It is rather a word for goodness, kindness, generosity
and love. St. John the Merciful, for example, was not a just
judge who showed mercy on criminals. He was a bishop who
distinguished himself as a helper and servant of the poor, the
lowly, the needy and the afflicted. The same man is sometimes
called St. John the Almsgiver.[1]

The word "mercy" in the English translation of *Kyrie
eleison* is from the Greek word *eleos,* which is most often, it
is true, translated as mercy. This word, however, comes from
the Hebrew word *hesed* which may be translated into English
in many different ways. Some Bibles say *mercy.*[2] Others say
steadfast love.[3] Still others say *tenderness* or *loving-kindness,*
or simply *love.*[4] The word also bears the connotation of gra-
ciousness, generosity, bounty and compassion. In the prayer
itself, of course, the original word is a verb and not a noun.
So it may as well be translated as "Lord, be merciful, gracious,
kind, generous, compassionate, bountiful, loving." According
to His self-revelation, God is all of these things, whether we
pray to Him or not. So when we pray, "Lord, have mercy,"
we are simply saying to God: Lord, be to us as You are!
Lord, act toward us as You do! Lord, we want You to be
with us and to do with us as You Yourself are and actually
do!

Having mercy is God's most distinguishing characteristic.
Pouring out His mercy, His steadfast love, upon His cove-
nanted people is His main occupation. Mercy is at the heart
of everything that God is and does and gives to His people.
It is the people's most treasured possession. The psalms, for
example, describe the steadfast love of the Lord, which is
the *mercy* of our prayer, in numberless ways. The steadfast
love of the Lord is from everlasting and endures forever. It

[1]This saint, patriarch of Alexandria, is commemorated on November 12.
[2]King James Version.
[3]Revised Standard Version.
[4]Jerusalem Bible.

is higher and greater than the heavens, yet the earth is full of this steadfast love, and it extends to the heavens. The Lord wakes His people up in the morning with it and surrounds them with it all the day long. It goes before them and follows them all the days of their lives. It preserves them and saves them. Through the steadfast love of the Lord, the people cut off their enemies and reign victorious in battle. The Christ is anointed with it, as are all the prophets, priests and kings. It leads the people in procession and takes them into the house of the Lord for worship. It crowns the people and blesses them, sanctifies and anoints them. The people contemplate the steadfast love of the Lord always. It is in their hearts, on their lips, at their right hands, before their eyes all the day and night. They rejoice in the steadfast love of the Lord, take pleasure and delight in it. It is their greatest treasure and most prized possession. For the people of God, the steadfast love of the Lord is better than life itself.

> O God, Thou art my God, I seek Thee,
>   my soul thirsts for Thee;
> my flesh faints for Thee,
>   as in a dry and weary land where no water is.
> So I have looked upon Thee in the sanctuary,
>   beholding Thy power and glory.
> Because Thy steadfast love is better than life,
>   my lips will praise Thee.
> So I will bless Thee as long as I live;
>   I will lift up my hands and call on Thy name.
>   (Ps. 63:1-4)

> Be mindful of Thy mercy, O Lord, and of Thy
>   steadfast love,
>   for they have been from of old.
> Remember not the sins of my youth, or my transgressions;
>   according to Thy steadfast love remember me,
>   for Thy goodness' sake, O Lord!
> Good and upright is the Lord;
>   therefore He instructs sinners in the way.
> He leads the humble in what is right,

and teaches the humble His way.
All the paths of the Lord are steadfast love and
    faithfulness,
    for those who keep His covenant and His testimonies.
      (Ps. 25:6-10)

Behold, the eye of the Lord is on those who fear Him,
    on those who hope in His steadfast love,
that He may deliver their soul from death,
    and keep them alive in famine.
Our soul waits for the Lord;
    He is our help and shield.
Yea, our heart is glad in Him,
    because we trust in His holy name.
Let Thy steadfast love, O Lord, be upon us,
    even as we hope in Thee. (Ps. 33:18-22)[5]

[5]The *steadfast love* in these citations is the *mercy* of the prayer, "Lord, have mercy." If the RSV had been in fashion when liturgical translations were first made in English, we might well be singing in our churches today: "Lord, have steadfast love."

16

Lord, Teach Us to Pray

When the disciples asked Jesus to teach them to pray, the Lord did not tell them to use their imaginations and express their feelings. He did not tell them that it really did not matter how they prayed, as long as they were sincere. And He certainly did not tell them to talk to God in their own words.

> He was praying in a certain place, and when He ceased, one of His disciples said to Him, "Lord, teach us to pray, as John taught his disciples." And He said to them, "When you pray, say: Father, hallowed be Thy name. Thy kingdom come. Give us each day our daily bread; and forgive us our sins, for we ourselves forgive every one who is indebted to us; and lead us not into temptation." (Lk. 11:1-4)

The Gospel according to St. Matthew also gives Jesus' teaching on prayer. This Gospel contains the version of the Lord's Prayer which is used liturgically by all Christians.

> And when you pray, you must not be like the hypocrites; for they love to stand and pray in the synagogues and at the street corners, that they may be seen by men. Truly, I say to you, they have received their reward. But when you pray, go into your room and shut the door and pray to your Father who is in secret; and your Father who sees in secret will reward you.

And in praying do not heap up empty phrases as
the Gentiles do; for they think that they will be heard
for their many words. Do not be like them, for your
Father knows what you need before you ask Him. Pray
then like this: Our Father who art in heaven, hallowed
be Thy name. Thy kingdom come, Thy will be done,
on earth as it is in heaven. Give us this day our daily
bread; and forgive us our debts, as we also have forgiven our debtors; and lead us not into temptation, but
deliver us from evil. (Mt. 6:5-13)

Jesus Christ prayed and taught His disciples to pray.
Prayer is at the heart of the Christian life. It is what demon-
strates that a person believes. And the Lord's Prayer is at the
heart of Christian prayer. All other prayers of the Church
exist in relation to this prayer given by the Master Himself.
They are either abbreviations or elaborations of it. They are
in harmony with it, and cannot contradict it in any way.

The fact that the Lord's Prayer is given in the scriptures
in two forms proves that it is not the words of the prayer,
even the Lord's Prayer, but the *content* of it that is of essential importance. Leo Tolstoy tells a story, probably taken from
Russian tradition, about three elders who were very holy, but
who could not remember the words of the Lord's Prayer.[1]
The point of the story is not that the Lord's Prayer is not
important, but that people may pray what the Lord's Prayer
says without knowing or being able to remember the exact
words. Those who wish to pray properly, however—whatever
their words or lack of words—must pray in spirit what the
Lord's Prayer intends. When they pray using words, the
words of the Lord's Prayer must be those which lie at the
center of their practice.

The saints of the Church warn against praying in ways
which contradict the Lord's Prayer. They say that people who
pray for things which are not specifically in the Lord's

[1]The story of Tolstoy is usually entitled "The Three Hermits." In it a
bishop attempts to teach the Lord's Prayer to three shining elders who live
alone on an island. They forget the words of the prayer and run over the
surface of the water after the bishop's boat to ask his forgiveness and if he
would please repeat the prayer once more.

Prayer insult their Master. This is an important warning of the Church's tradition, to be especially heeded in the time of Great Lent. St. John Cassian concluded his commentary on the Lord's Prayer, one of the earliest in the Church's history available to us, with these powerful words:

> You see then what is the method and form of prayer proposed to us by the Judge Himself, Who is prayed to by it. It is a form which contains no petition for riches, no thought of honors, no request for power and might, no mention of bodily health and of temporal life. For He Who is the Author of Eternity would have people ask Him nothing uncertain, nothing paltry, nothing temporal. And so a person will offer the greatest insult to His Majesty and Bounty if he leaves on one side these eternal petitions and chooses rather to ask of Him something transitory and uncertain. And he will also incur the indignation rather than the propitiation of the Judge through the pettiness of his prayer.[2]

The Church herself reminds us of the centrality of the Lord's Prayer:

> Come, let us gather in the chamber of our soul,
> rendering prayers to the Lord and crying:
> "Our Father, who art in heaven,
> forgive and remit our transgressions,
> since You alone are compassionate."
>
> Let us serve the Lord with fear.
> Let us anoint our heads with the oil of good deeds.
> Let us wash our faces with the waters of purity.
> Let us not use empty phrases in prayer,
> but as we have been taught, let us cry out:
> "Our Father, who art in heaven,
> forgive us our trespasses,
> for You are the Lover of man."[3]

[2]St. John Cassian, *The First Conference of Abbot Isaac: On Prayer,* chapter 24. [3]First Tuesday matins.

17

Seek First His Kingdom

During Great Lent we try to do what we should be doing all the time. The lenten season, therefore, is most particularly the time for seeking the Kingdom of God. This is the teaching of Jesus.

> "Therefore I tell you, do not be anxious about your life, what you shall eat or what you shall drink, nor about your body, what you shall put on. Is not life more than food, and the body more than clothing? . . . Therefore do not be anxious, saying, 'What shall we eat?' or 'What shall we drink?' or 'What shall we wear?' For the Gentiles seek all these things; and your heavenly Father knows that you need them all. But seek first His kingdom and His righteousness, and all these things shall be yours as well." (Mt. 6:25, 31-33)

One of the greatest tragedies today is that people who call themselves Christians present the Christian faith and life in ways directly opposed to the teaching of the Lord. They not only imply but openly proclaim that God exists to make life go better for His followers in this world. They say that you can come before God and "name it and claim it." Health, wealth, happiness, prosperity in this world are what, according to them, the Lord primarily promises and provides. All this and heaven too!

It is certainly true that the Lord loves His faithful people and cares for them. Indeed, He loves and cares for everyone, including the wicked, the selfish and the ungrateful (see Lk.

6:35). But a faithful follower of Christ who loves God the Father and is filled with His Holy Spirit will never come to Him looking for the good things of this life. He will come seeking the Kingdom of God which, according to St. Paul, is "not food and drink but righteousness and peace and joy in the Holy Spirit" (Rom. 14:17). And while seeking the Kingdom, he knows that he will get whatever else he needs as well. But he leaves that up to the Lord.

Commenting on the Lord's Prayer, St. Isaac the Syrian gives the same teaching that we found in St. John Cassian. It is filled with warnings which we must heed and obey.

> Do not be inept in your petitions lest you grieve God by your ignorance. Learn to pray properly, that you may be esteemed worthy of glorious things. Seek from Him what is really valuable; He will not withhold them. Then you will receive honor from Him because of the choice of your wise will.

> The honor of the King is diminished by those who seek from Him contemptible things.

> When a man seeks from a king a measure full of dung, he will not only be despised by his despicable request, exposing thus his ignorance, but he also insults the king by his insipid demand. Such also is he who asks corporeal things from God.

> Do not seek from God that which He is anxious to give us even when we do not beg for it, which He does not withhold even from those who are wholly alien to any knowledge of Him and even do not know that He exists. Do not use vain repetitions as the pagans do . . . and give no thought saying "What shall we eat, or what shall we drink, or with what shall we be clothed?" Your Father knows that you also have need of all these things.

> If your Father takes care of the birds . . . how much

more will He take care of you? But ask from God the Kingdom and righteousness, then He will add these things too.

And if He is slow in granting your request, and you ask without receiving promptly, do not be distressed. For you are not wiser than God. When you remain spiritually as you are, it is either because your behavior does not agree with your request, or because the ways of your heart diverge from the aims of your prayer, or because your inner state is childish in comparison with the greatness of the things of God. It is not fitting that the great things of God should fall into our hands easily, lest the gift of God be thought to be of little worth because it is acquired without difficulty. All that is gathered by labor is guarded with care.

Thirst after Jesus. Then He will satisfy you with His love. Shut your eyes to the precious things of this world, then you will be deemed worthy of the peace given by God to reign in your heart. Restrain yourself from the allurements that are shining before your eyes, then you will be deemed worthy yourself to shine with spiritual joy.[1]

As the Church teaches us to sing:

Having despised the satisfaction of passions, my
    humble soul,
be nourished by the food of good deeds.
Take joy in the sweetness of fasting,
avoiding the woe of earthly sweetness,
and be enriched forever.

My soul is blinded, darkened by the drunkenness
    of passion;
in no way can I look to Thee, O God.

[1]St. Isaac of Syria, *Third Treatise on the Behavior of Excellence.*

Therefore, be bountiful to me and enlighten me
and open to me the gates of true repentance.[2]

Become as lightning, O my soul.
Receive the flashing rays of abstinence,
and flee the darkness of sin,
that through the divine Spirit of God
the light of forgiveness may enlighten you as the
   rising sun.[3]

[2]First Monday matins.
[3]First Thursday matins.

18

O Lord and Master of My Life

The lenten prayer *par excellence* in the Orthodox Church is the prayer of St. Ephraim of Syria.[1] It is chanted at every lenten service, sometimes more than once.[2] For many people, the spirit of Lent, the very breath of the lenten spring, is contained in this brief prayer.

O Lord and Master of my life,
take from me the spirit of sloth, despair, lust of power
    and idle talk,
but grant rather the spirit of chastity, humility, patience
    and love to Thy servant.
Yea, O Lord and King,
grant me to see my own transgressions and not to
    judge my brother,
for blessed art Thou, unto ages of ages. Amen.

The prayer of St. Ephraim is translated into English in many different ways. Almost all mistranslate the first sentence, as we have quoted above.[3] The prayer does not say "take from me" the spirit of sloth. It says rather "do not give to

[1]St. Ephraim lived in the fourth century. Some say that he was a deacon, ordained by St. Basil the Great; others say he was a priest.

[2]The prayer of St. Ephraim is not used at the services of Saturday and Sunday during the Great Fast because these services are not lenten in character, being the Sabbath and the Lord's Day. For this reason some people are ignorant of the prayer. It is used twice in the Liturgy of the Presanctified Gifts in the Slavic traditions, though it is often not used at this liturgy in the Byzantine practice.

[3]The translation here is from the lenten books of the Orthodox Church in America.

me." This small point is an important one. It reminds us that everything is from God, good things and bad. It underscores the critical fact that even the evil spirits, and not only the good, are in God's hands. It emphasizes the truth that God is the God of everything: light and darkness, good and evil, angels and devils, life and death. All things are in God's hands, and He is the Lord over all.

In the holy scriptures there are many instances when the point is made that everything that comes to a person is from God, even tempting things and troubles, wicked things and evil, sinful things and death itself. This is hard for modern people, including many Christians, to comprehend and accept. But it is, nevertheless, the teaching. This does not mean that God Himself tempts people and forces evil upon them and makes them to be wicked, "for God cannot be tempted with evil," says the letter of James, "and He Himself tempts no one; but each person is tempted when he is lured and enticed by his own desire. Then desire when it has conceived gives birth to sin; and sin when it is full-grown brings forth death" (Jas. 1:13-15). God tempts no one. But when a person is tempted by the devil and his own desire, God allows it. And in a real sense, He does more than allow it. He causes it. He gives it. He brings it about.

This is the clear teaching of the Bible. It is found in such shocking declarations in the Old Testament as this: "The Spirit of the Lord departed from Saul, and an evil spirit from the Lord tormented him" (1 Sam. 16:14). It is found also in the prophets, when God Himself declares concerning His people:

> . . . I gave them statutes that were not good and ordinances by which they could not have life; and I defiled them through their very gifts in making them offer by fire all their first-born, that I might horrify them; I did it that they might know that I am the Lord. (Ezek. 20:25-26)

This teaching is found in the New Testament scriptures as well. The apostle Paul writes concerning the wicked that

"God gave them up in the lusts of their hearts to impurity
. . . God gave them up to dishonorable passions . . . God
gave them up to a base mind and to improper conduct" (Rom.
1:24, 26, 28); "God sends upon them a strong delusion, to
make them believe what is false, so that all may be condemned who did not believe the truth but had pleasure in
unrighteousness" (2 Thess. 2:11-12).

The teaching seems to be this: If we want evil spirits,
God gives them. If we want demons to destroy us, God sends
them. If we want to be tempted by our own passionate lusts
and desires, God will give us over to them and surrender us
to their defiling and destructive power. And so we pray: O
Lord and Master of our life, do not give us the spirit of sloth,
despair, lust of power and idle talk, but give rather the spirit
of chastity, humility, patience and love to Your servants. Do
not give us over to our sinful passions and desires which
defile and destroy us, but give us Your Holy Spirit to fill us
with His numberless graces and fruits. You are the Lord.
The demons are subject to Your power. Life and death are
in Your hands. You kill and You make alive. You cast down
and You raise up again. You make poor and make rich. You
bring low and also exalt. All things are Your servants. Lead
us not into temptation, O Lord, but deliver us from the evil
one.

> For the Lord will vindicate His people
>   and have compassion on His servants,
> when He sees that their power is gone,
>   and there is none remaining, bond or free.
> Then He will say, "Where are their gods,
>   the rock in which they took refuge,
> who ate the fat of their sacrifices,
>   and drank the wine of their drink offering?
> Let them rise up and help you,
>   let them be your protection!
> See now that I, even I, am He;
>   and there is no god beside me;
> I kill and I make alive;
>   I wound and I heal;

and there is none that can deliver out of my hand."
    (Deut. 32:36-39)[4]

O my gracious Savior,
be my Healer and Redeemer,
and cast me not away.
Raise me up when You see me fallen,
    lying in sin,
since You are all-powerful,
that I may know Your deeds and cry
    out to You:
"Before I perish completely,
    save me, O Lord!"[5]

19

The Wiles of the Devil

The prayers of the Church are filled with references to the devil. The Lord's own prayer ends with the petition: Deliver us from the evil one![1] The life of a person who wills to be with God and to live in His Kingdom is, by definition, a life of struggle against the devil and his armies of evil spirits. The lenten season is especially the time for waging this spiritual battle.

One cannot read the Bible without being reminded that the evil spirits exist and wage fierce warfare against those who love God. Jesus Himself said that He "saw Satan fall like lightning from heaven" (Lk. 10:18).[2] He cast out many evil spirits as an essential sign of His messiahship. And He gave this power to His disciples as well, warning them to be watchful and attentive in their spiritual lives lest they too be led astray by the evil spirits. At the end of the ages, Jesus teaches, the wicked shall enter into "eternal punishment" by being cast "into the eternal fire prepared for the devil and his angels" (Mt. 25:46, 41). And the apostles of Christ give the very same teaching.

"Put on the whole armor of God," the apostle Paul commands, "that you may be able to stand against the wiles of

[1]The "evil" at the end of the Lord's Prayer may be interpreted as evil in general, or the specific evil of the "last times" which attacks God's elect. It also may be interpreted (as it is by St. John Cassian, St. John Chrysostom and others) as the "evil one," that is, the devil.

[2]Satan means "adversary" or "enemy." The devil in the scriptures and in the Church's liturgy is also called "the deceiver" and "the liar." See Jesus' explanation of the parable of the weeds in the field: "the enemy who sowed them is the devil" (Mt. 13:24-43; also Jn. 8:39-47). According to St. Paul, "Satan disguises himself as an angel of light" (2 Cor. 11:14).

the devil. For we are not contending against flesh and blood, but against the principalities, against the powers, against the world rulers of this present darkness, against the spiritual hosts of wickedness in the heavenly places" (Eph. 6:11-12).[3] A letter ascribed to the apostle Peter warns: "Be sober, be watchful. Your adversary the devil prowls around like a roaring lion, seeking some one to devour. Resist him, firm in your faith, knowing that the same experience of suffering is required of your brotherhood throughout the world" (1 Pet. 5:8-9).

All of the saints of the Church had direct spiritual contact with the devil and the host of evil spirits. Not one saint has escaped this conscious confrontation. Those who went off alone into the desert to battle with Satan face to face, on his own territory so to speak—for the traditional idea was that the barren wastelands were the special habitations of evil spirits—had especially vivid and violent experiences. It could not be otherwise, since there was little or nothing at all in the wilderness through which the devil could tempt and ensnare them. He had to attack directly and openly, with all of his wiles.

St. Anthony the Great is known for his particularly vicious battles with the evil spirits. In letters attributed to this "father of fathers" among the ascetic saints, we find the following testimony about the actions of the evil ones:[4]

> I want you to know, my children, that I cease not
> to pray God for you night and day, that He may open
> for you the eyes of your hearts to see the many hidden
> malignities which the evil spirits pour upon us daily.
> I want God to give you a heart of knowledge and a

[3]Some people interpret the biblical "principalities and powers" as political and economic powers in this world. These are, however, actually names for angels, both good and bad. See Col. 1:15-16 and 2:10-15.

[4]St. Anthony the Great is called the "father of fathers" in the Church's liturgical commemoration of January 17. He lived in the fourth century. Though he was not the first to go to the desert, he is considered the founder of the monastic way in the Christian Church. His life was written by St. Athanasius the Great, whom he supported in his defense of the divinity of the Son of God.

spirit of discernment, that you may be able to offer
your hearts as a pure sacrifice before the Father, in
great holiness, without blemish. Truly my children,
they envy us at all times, with their evil counsel, and
hidden persecution, and subtle malice, and spirit of
seduction, and their blasphemous thoughts, and their
hardening of heart, and their many griefs which they
bring upon us at every hour, and the faintings which
they make our heart to faint daily, and all the anger
and mutual slander which they teach us, and the self-
justifications in what we do, and the judgments which
they set in our hearts, causing us . . . to judge our
fellows . . . and the contempt which they set in our
hearts by pride, when we are hard-hearted and despise
each other, when we are bitter against each other with
our hard words, grieving at every hour, accusing each
other and not ourselves, thinking that our toil is from
our fellows, sitting in judgment on what appears out-
wardly, while the robber is all within our house [i.e.,
the devil is in us]; and the disputes and divisions
wherein we dispute against each other until we estab-
lish our own way, to appear justified in the face of
each other.

The evil spirits make us jealous for works which
we are not able to accomplish, and cause us to faint in
tasks in which we are engaged, and which are profitable for us. They make us laugh when it is time for
weeping and weep when it is time for laughter, and
simply turn us aside at every time from the right way.
. . . But when they fill our heart with these deceits, and
we feed on them and they become our food, then God
is patient with us and He comes to us to bring us back
again. . . . Therefore weary not of praying the goodness of the Father, if perchance His help may come
upon you, that you may teach yourselves to know what
is right. . . .

In truth, my children, I tell you that every person
who delights in his own will, and is subdued to his
own thoughts, and takes up the things sown in his

heart, and rejoices in them, and supposes in his heart that these are some great chosen mystery and justifies himself in what he does—the soul of such a man is a lair of evil spirits, counseling him to evil, and his body a store of evil mysteries which it hides in itself: and over such a one the demons have great power, because he has not dishonored them before all men. . . .

For they know that our perdition is from our neighbor, and our life also from our neighbor. . . . For this cause, therefore, he who sins against his neighbor sins against himself, and he who does evil to his neighbor does evil to himself; and he who does good to his neighbor does good to himself. . . . Therefore, let us rouse up God in ourselves by support of one another, and deliver ourselves to death for our souls and for each other; and if we do this, we shall be manifesting the very substance of God's compassion for us. Let us not be lovers of ourselves so as not to become subject to the power of evil spirits.[5]

Near to our own time, St. Seraphim of Sarov, who also dwelt alone for decades in the wilderness and in monastic enclosure, taught that "the temptations of the devil are like a cobweb. You only need to blow at it, and it will be destroyed. It is the same with our enemy, the devil. You only need to shield yourself with the sign of the Holy Cross, and all his wiles will vanish completely." And when asked if he had ever seen evil spirits the saint replied simply with a smile, "They are hideous! Just as it is impossible for a sinner to look upon an angel, so it is a horrible thing to see the devils. They are hideous!"[6]

Attending the bright and joyful banquet of the Fast,
we cry aloud: "Keep us in peace, O Lord,
destroying every wile of the enemy;
and make us worthy, as You are supremely good,

[5]St. Anthony, *Letter VI*.
[6]St. Seraphim of Sarov died in 1833 and was canonized in 1903. He is considered among the greatest of Russian saints.

to greet Your precious Cross in fear,
through which You grant great mercy to the world,
for You alone are merciful!"[7]

O great wonder!
I behold the Tree on which Christ was crucified in
    the flesh,
and the world enlightened through its adoration, crying:
"O the power of the Cross!
The demons see it and are burned;
by its sign they are consumed with flames."
Therefore I bless you, O pure tree of the Cross.
I honor and adore you with awe,
glorifying God who through you grants me
    unending life.[8]

[7]Third Wednesday matins.
[8]Third Sunday vespers.

20

My Soul, My Soul—Arise!

The lenten season is a time for labor and effort. It is a season when we strive to energize ourselves, to wake ourselves up, to motivate ourselves to spiritual feats. It is a time when we declare a conscious struggle against sloth, and beg the Lord not to give us this evil spirit, but to take it from us when we are caught in its snares.

My soul, my soul—arise!
Why are you sleeping?
The end is at hand;
destruction hangs over you.
Come again to your senses
that you may be spared by Christ our God,
who is everywhere, filling all things.[1]

During Lent the book of Proverbs is read at vespers each evening. One of its main teachings is about the slothful person, the sluggard, the one who is spiritually and physically lazy and lethargic, unmotivated and impotent.

Go to the ant, O sluggard;
    consider her ways, and be wise.
Without having any chief, officer or ruler,
    she prepares her food in summer,
        and gathers her sustenance in harvest.
How long will you lie there, O sluggard?
    When will you arise from your sleep? (Prov. 6:6-9)

[1]Kontakion of the Canon of St. Andrew of Crete.

As a door turns on its hinges,
    so does a sluggard on his bed.
The sluggard buries his hand in the dish;
    it wears him out to bring it back to his mouth.
The sluggard is wiser in his own eyes
    than seven men who can answer discreetly.
        (Prov. 26:14-16)

The apostle Paul is clear in his writings about Christians who will not work. His teaching is strong and insistent.

> Now we command you, brethren, in the name of our Lord Jesus Christ, that you keep away from any brother who is living in idleness and not in accord with the tradition that you received from us. For you yourselves know how you ought to imitate us; we were not idle when we were with you, we did not eat any one's bread without paying, but with toil and labor we worked night and day, that we might not burden any of you. It was not because we have not that right, but to give you in our conduct an example to imitate. For even when we were with you, we gave you this command: If any one will not work, let him not eat. For we hear that some of you are living in idleness, mere busybodies, not doing any work. Now such persons we command and exhort in the Lord Jesus Christ to do their work in quietness and to earn their own living. Brethren, do not be weary in well-doing. If any one refuses to obey what we say in this letter, note that man, and have nothing to do with him, that he may be ashamed. Do not look on him as an enemy, but warn him as a brother. (2 Thess. 3:6-15)

A person who loves the Lord and lives with Him will never be idle. He will always be working. He will never be spiritually weary in well-doing, for he does not labor by his own efforts and powers but by the grace and strength of his Master. Thus, a person who is spiritually exhausted is the gravest of sinners. For, as Isaiah says, whose prophecy is read at each service of the sixth hour during Great Lent, God almighty does not faint or grow weary, and He gives this power to those who faithfully serve Him.

> Have you not known? Have you not heard?
> The Lord is the everlasting God,
>> the Creator of the ends of the earth.
> He does not faint or grow weary,
>> His understanding is unsearchable.
> He gives power to the faint,
>> and to him who has no might He increases strength.
> Even youths shall faint and be weary,
>> and young men shall fall exhausted;
> but they who wait for the Lord shall renew their strength,
>> they shall mount up with wings like eagles,
> they shall run and not be weary,
>> they shall walk and not faint. (Is. 40:28-31)

During Great Lent we work to wake up and to overcome our weariness. We labor to come alive and to conquer our laziness. We strive to come to our senses and to displace the spirit of sloth with the uncreated energies of God which are given through His Spirit to those who love Him.

> The arena of virtues has been opened!
> Let all who wish to struggle for the prize enter now.
> Let them gird themselves for the noble contest of the Fast,
> for those who strive rightly are justly crowned.
> Let us take up the armor of the Cross and make war
>> against the Enemy.
> Let the faith be our invincible weapon.
> Let prayer be our shield and almsgiving our helmet.
> Let us use fasting as a sword to cut away all evil from
>> our hearts.
> If we do this, we shall receive the true crown on
>> judgment day from Christ the King of all.[2]

---

[2] Cheesefare Sunday matins.

21

Men of Violence Take It by Force

The Prayer of St. Ephraim begs God to keep us from the spirit of despondency and despair. This particular vice, which goes together with laziness, lethargy and sloth in the lenten prayer, is very hard to translate and define. It is sometimes rendered as faintheartedness. It may also be translated as listlessness. It does not mean simply to be without hope, which is what "despair" literally means. It is rather to be timid, weak, without courage, without spiritual strength, without motivation. It means, in modern slang, to be a "blah" person, incapable of courageous action and daring spiritual exploits. One infected with this disease is sometimes described in the tradition as being stricken with insensibility and insensitivity. He is a person who moans, sighs, groans, stares out the window, sighs again, pities himself, complains about others, gripes about everything, and returns again and again to wallow in his spiritual misery, sterility and impotence. St. John Climacus describes him in this way:

> He talks about healing a wound, and does not stop irritating it. He complains of sickness, and does not stop eating what is harmful. He prays against it, and immediately goes and does it. And when he has done it, he is angry with himself; and the wretched man is not ashamed of his own words. "I am doing wrong," he cries, and eagerly continues to do so. His mouth prays against his passion, and his body struggles for it. He philosophizes about death, but he behaves as if he were immortal. He groans over the separation of

soul and body, but drowses along as if he were eternal. He talks of temperance and self-control, but he lives for gluttony. He reads about the judgment and begins to smile. He reads about vainglory, and is vainglorious while actually reading. He repeats what he has learnt about vigil, and drops asleep on the spot. He praises prayer, but runs from it as from the plague. He blesses obedience, but he is the first to disobey. He praises detachment, but he is not ashamed to be spiteful and to fight for a rag. When angered he gets bitter, and he is angered again at his bitterness; and he does not feel that after one defeat he is suffering another. Having overeaten he repents, and a little later again gives way to it. He blesses silence, and praises it with a spate of words. He teaches meekness, and during the actual teaching frequently gets angry. Having woken from passion he sighs, and shaking his head, he again yields to passion. He condemns laughter, and lectures on mourning with a smile on his face. Before others he blames himself for being vainglorious, and in blaming himself is only angling for glory for himself. He looks people in the face with passion, and talks about chastity. While frequenting the world, he praises the solitary life, without realizing that he shames himself. He extols almsgivers, and reviles beggars. All the time he is his own accuser, and he does not want to come to his senses—I will not say cannot.[1]

The vicious disease of insensitive despondency is healed, according to the scriptures and the saints, only when one really wills to be cured and is ready to do what is necessary for healing. First of all he must realize the violence of the effort needed, for "the kingdom of heaven has suffered violence," Jesus says, "and men of violence take it by force" (Mt. 11:12).

The law and the prophets were until John [the Baptist]; since then the good news [the gospel] of

[1]*The Ladder of Divine Ascent*, step 18.

the kingdom of God is preached, and every one enters
it violently. (Lk. 16:16)

The struggle is real. It is violent. It is not for cowards or
weaklings. One must stand in the struggle, and do everything
to stand, by the grace and power of God which come to us
through faith and hope which are received and strengthened
by prayer and abstinence and fasting, wakefulness and vigil.
It is a struggle unto death for eternal life with God. The
apostle Paul once again has the adequate words:

> Therefore take the whole armor of God, that you may
> be able to withstand in the evil day, and having done
> all, to stand. Stand therefore, having girded your loins
> with truth, and having put on the breastplate of right-
> eousness, and having shod your feet with the equip-
> ment of the gospel of peace; besides all these, taking
> the shield of faith, with which you can quench all the
> flaming darts of the evil one. And take the helmet of
> salvation, and the sword of the Spirit, which is the
> word of God. Pray at all times in the Spirit, with all
> prayer and supplication. To that end keep alert with
> all perseverance, making supplication for all the saints
> ... (Eph. 6:13-18)

Desiring to commune with the divine Pascha,
the Pascha not from Egypt but from Zion,
let us renounce the drink of sin through repentance.
Let us gird our loins with the mortification of pleasures.
Let us cover our feet with shoes that tread no evil path.
Let us be confirmed with the shield of faith.
Let us not imitate the enemies of the Master's Cross.
Let us pursue victory over the devil by fasting,
for the sake of our Savior who has shown us the way![2]

---

[2]First Thursday vespers.

22

Not to Be Served, but to Serve

The lenten prayer of St. Ephraim petitions the Lord
against the spirit of lust of power. For it to have been included
in this supplication, this spirit must be one which applies to
everyone in a particularly subtle and crafty way.

Why should we pray against lust of power? We are not
great and important people. There is little temptation for
us to wield authority and to exercise force. There is little
chance that we can lord it over others and exert our ideas and
desires. We are normal people, regular folks, plain and
simple. Or so we think.

The fact is that we exercise authority and wield power
all the time: in our homes, in our churches, in our work, in
society generally. And even if this power were small and
of little effect—though it is not at all—we could still fall
victim to lusting after the ability to get our own way, to do
what we want, to impose our own ideas, to enact our own
programs, to manipulate others, and to have them in our
control. We do this all the time, and we are usually not even
aware of it. If we would just examine our thoughts through
the course of a day, however, and analyse our involvement
in things, we would be convinced of it. We desire to enforce
our will and to get our way in almost everything we do.

Jesus Christ has all authority in heaven and on earth. He
has it eternally as the Son and Word of God by whom all
things are created and in whom all things hold together.[1]
And He has earned it as a man when, coming on earth in

[1]See Jn. 1:1-5; Heb. 1:1-4; Col. 1:15-19.

human flesh, He humbled Himself in obedience to His Father
unto death for the sake of the world's salvation.

Jesus has all power and authority. He can call legions
of angels and wipe out the entire universe (Mt. 26:53; Jn.
19:10-11). But He does not do this. Instead He reveals what
power and authority really are in their divine content and
perfect expression by serving His Father and His people, and
by loving them "to the end" (Jn. 13:1).

> When He had washed their feet, and taken His gar-
> ments, and resumed His place, He said to them, "Do
> you know what I have done to you? You call me
> Teacher and Lord; and you are right, for so I am. If I
> then, your Lord and Teacher, have washed your feet,
> you also ought to wash one another's feet. For I have
> given you an example, that you also should do as I
> have done to you. Truly, truly, I say to you, a servant
> is not greater than his master; nor is he who is sent
> greater than he who sent him. If you know these things,
> blessed are you if you do them." (Jn. 13:12-17)

> And Jesus called them to Him and said to them, "You
> know that those who are supposed to rule over the
> Gentiles lord it over them, and their great men exercise
> authority over them. But it shall not be so among you;
> but whoever would be great among you must be your
> servant, and whoever would be first among you must be
> slave of all. For the Son of man also came not to be
> served but to serve, and to give His life as a ransom
> for many." (Mk. 10:42-45)[2]

Human beings are created to imitate the loving humility
of God Himself, the divine service revealed to the world in
the person of Jesus, the Son of God in human flesh. The
disciples of Jesus are called to imitate their Master and Lord
in His self-emptying sacrifice of love upon the Cross.

---

[2]This is from the gospel reading at the divine liturgy of the Fifth Sunday
of Lent.

Have this mind among yourselves, which is yours in Christ Jesus, who, though He was in the form of God, did not count equality with God a thing to be grasped, but emptied Himself, taking the form of a servant, being born in the likeness of men. And being found in human form He humbled Himself and became obedient unto death, even death on a cross. Therefore God has highly exalted Him and bestowed on Him the name which is above every name, that at the name of Jesus every knee should bow, in heaven and on earth and under the earth, and every tongue confess that Jesus Christ is Lord, to the glory of God the Father. (Phil. 2:5-11)[3]

In the rock opera *Jesus Christ Superstar* there is at least one good scene. The people are screaming at Jesus to show His power and authority in signs and wonders and miracles for their benefit. Jesus cuts them off, and in a soft and gentle voice declares: "Neither you Simon, nor the fifty thousand, nor the Romans, nor the Jews, nor Judas, nor the Twelve, nor the priests, nor the scribes, nor doomed Jerusalem itself, understand what power is, understand what glory is, understand at all, understand at all. . . ."

Do we yet understand? Do we understand anything at all? Do we see, and want to see, that power and glory are to obey God and to seek His will in order to do it? Do we see and believe that power is fulfilled in meekness, and authority in service? Do we comprehend and accept the fact that the Author of Life Himself, Jesus the Son of God, being made like us His brethren in every respect, being tempted as we are tempted in order to be with us in our temptations, was Himself made perfect as a man through what He suffered for our sake? (See Heb. 2:10-18.[4]) Are we yet persuaded by this vision? Are we yet convinced of this logic? Are we yet ready

---

[3]This famous passage of St. Paul is the epistle reading at the divine liturgies of the Nativity, Dormition and Protection of the Virgin Mary.

[4]The letter to the Hebrews provides the epistle readings at all of the divine liturgies during Great Lent, which means each Saturday and Sunday, and the feast of the Annunciation. The passage referred to here is the reading for Annunciation.

to learn from Him who is "gentle and lowly in heart," to
take His yoke upon ourselves so that we may find rest for
our souls? (See Mt. 11:28-30.) These are questions which the
lenten season asks us every day.

You manifested humility, O Christ,
as the way of genuine nobility
by emptying Yourself and taking the form of a slave.
You did not hear the self-praising prayers of the Pharisee,
but you received the broken sighs of the publican as
     a blameless sacrifice.
Therefore I cry out to You:
"Have mercy on me, O God, have mercy on me,
and save me, O Savior."[5]

We venerate Your most pure image, O Good One,
and ask forgiveness of our transgressions, O Christ
     our God.
Of Your good will You were pleased to ascend the
     Cross in the flesh,
and to deliver Your creatures from bondage to the Enemy.
Therefore with thankfulness we cry out to You:
"With joy have You filled all things, O our Savior,
in that You have come to save the world."[6]

[5]Fourth Monday matins.
[6]The troparion of the First Sunday of Great Lent, the Sunday of the
feast of the Triumph of Orthodoxy. It is also sung on the feast of the Icon-
not-made-by-hands on August 16, the temple feast of churches dedicated to
Christ the Savior. And it forms part of the rite of the clergy's entrance into
the sanctuary for the celebration of the holy Eucharist.

23

The Tongue is a Fire

The lenten Prayer of St. Ephraim begs God to free His servants from the sin of idle talk. This evil is also called vain babbling and empty chatter. It is the wickedness of the noise pollution of words devoid of meaning and purpose; words which cannot comfort, encourage, edify, instruct, inspire or inform. The point here is clear. It is not only evil and wicked words which are sinful. It is idle and empty words as well; words which may well be true, but need not be spoken. Jesus says that we shall answer at the last judgment for our words.

Either make the tree good, and its fruit good; or make the tree bad, and its fruit bad; for the tree is known by its fruit. You brood of vipers! how can you speak good, when you are evil? For out of the abundance of the heart the mouth speaks. The good man out of his good treasure brings forth good, and the evil man out of his evil treasure brings forth evil. I tell you, on that day of judgment men will render account for every careless word they utter; for by your words you will be justified, and by your words you will be condemned. (Mt. 12:33-37)[1]

The word is the human being's most prized possession. It is what distinguishes people from rocks and plants and animals. It is what shows them to be made in the image and likeness of God. Human beings can think and speak. They

[1]The word "careless" here may be translated as vain, void, empty and meaningless.

can express themselves and make themselves known. They
can bless God and sing His praises. They can utter His teachings and make known His ways. They can give thanks and
adore. But they can also curse and blaspheme, gossip and lie,
slander and condemn.

> If we put bits into the mouths of horses that they may
> obey us, we guide their whole bodies. Look at the ships
> also; though they are so great and are driven by strong
> winds, they are guided by a very small rudder
> wherever the will of the pilot directs. So the tongue is
> a little member and boasts of great things. How great
> a forest is set ablaze by a small fire! And the tongue
> is a fire. The tongue is an unrighteous world among
> our members, staining the whole body, setting on fire
> the cycle of nature, and set on fire by hell. For every
> kind of beast and bird, of reptile and sea creature, can
> be tamed and has been tamed by humankind, but no
> human being can tame the tongue—a restless evil, full
> of deadly poison. With it we bless the Lord and Father,
> and with it we curse men, who are made in the likeness
> of God. From the same mouth come blessing and
> cursing. My brethren, this ought not to be so. (Jas.
> 3:3-10)

The author of the second letter to Timothy warns Christians
"to avoid disputing about words, which does no good, but
only ruins the hearers." He urges them to "avoid such godless
chatter, for it will lead people into more and more ungodli-
ness, and their talk will eat its way like gangrene" (2 Tim.
2:14-17). The book of Proverbs, which is read at each lenten
vespers, provides the same instruction.

> My son, be attentive to my words;
>   incline your ear to my sayings.
> Let them not escape from your sight;
>   keep them within your heart.
> For they are life to him who finds them,
>   and healing to all his flesh.

Keep your heart with all vigilance;
 for from it flow the springs of life.
Put away from you crooked speech,
 and put devious talk far from you.
Let your eyes look directly forward,
 and your gaze be straight before you. (Prov. 4:20-25)

The mouth of the righteous is a fountain of life,
 but the mouth of the wicked conceals violence. . . .
He who heeds instruction is on the path to life,
 but he who rejects reproof goes astray.
He who conceals hatred has lying lips,
 and he who utters slander is a fool.
When words are many, transgression is not lacking,
 but he who restrains his lips is prudent.
The tongue of the righteous is choice silver;
 the mind of the wicked is of little worth.
The lips of the righteous feed many,
 but fools die for lack of sense. (Prov. 10:11, 17-21)

He who belittles his neighbor lacks sense,
 but a man of understanding remains silent.
He who goes about as a talebearer reveals secrets,
 but he who is trustworthy in spirit keeps a thing
  hidden. (Prov. 11:12-13)

A soft answer turns away wrath,
 but a harsh word stirs up anger.
The tongue of the wise dispenses knowledge,
 but the mouths of fools pour out folly.
The eyes of the Lord are in every place,
 keeping watch on the evil and the good.
A gentle tongue is a tree of life,
 but perverseness in it breaks the spirit. (Prov. 15:1-4)

These lines from Proverbs are but a taste of its teachings about words and silence, which may all be summed up in one psalm line that is solemnly chanted at each lenten vespers: "Set a watch, O Lord, about my mouth, and a door of enclosure about my lips" (Ps. 141:3).[2] People often repent of speaking, St. Ambrose of Milan observes in an often-quoted saying, but seldom of silence.[3] St. John Climacus says that "he who has become aware of his sins has controlled his tongue, but a talkative person has yet to know himself as he ought," since "he who cares for his salvation cuts down on words, while he who gains repentance shuns talkativeness like fire."[4]

> Let us present a Fast good and well-pleasing to the Lord.
> A true Fast is alienation from the Evil One,
> the holding of one's tongue,
> the laying aside of all anger,
> the removal of all sensuality,
> the casting aside of accusations, lies and sins of swearing.
> The dissipation of these makes the Fast true and
>   acceptable.[5]

---

[2]The translation here is that which is normally sung from service books of the Orthodox Church in America.
[3]Taken from the Life of St. Seraphim of Sarov.
[4]*The Ladder of Divine Ascent*, step 11.
[5]First Monday vespers.

24

To the Pure All Things Are Pure

The first petition in the lenten prayer of St. Ephraim is for the spirit of chastity. The word is an interesting one in the original language. It is a combination of the word for wholeness and integrity, and the word for wisdom and understanding. This basically is what chastity is: soundness and wholeness, completeness and sanity. It is not something physical or biological. It is not something negative, the indication of "something not happening." It is the positive quality of "having it all together" and "keeping it intact." It is a spiritual condition. It is the healthy integration and soundness of body, heart, mind and spirit. It is a fundamental and essential necessity for authentic life.

There is an obsession with sexuality in our time. We have come to idolize sexual activity. We virtually enthrone it in the place of God in our lives. We identify it as the cause of our happiness or sorrow, our fulfillment or dissatisfaction, our success or failure as human beings. We tend, though not always consciously and with clear awareness, to think that our identity, value and significance as persons are rooted in our sexual expressions and successes. This spirit is in the atmosphere. It is in the air we breathe. It flies like an aerial phantom through the skies, all too often making its voice heard and its image seen on the radios, television sets, phonographs and movie screens of our homes and theaters. It finds its way into our classrooms and counseling sessions. It enters even into our places of religious activity and devotion. It appears everywhere, filling all things with its poisonous deceit.

The Lord Jesus Christ was chaste. So was His mother Mary.

So was His greatest disciple and prophet, the one whom He called the greatest born of woman, the forerunner and baptizer John. If the Lord Jesus Christ, God's only Son, and the Virgin and the Baptist, His fully sanctified servants, were not the most perfectly fulfilled persons who ever lived on the earth, then Christianity is in very deep trouble. Indeed, it is hopelessly aberrant. It is a ludicrous farce.

> Do you not know that the unrighteous will not inherit the kingdom of God? Do not be deceived; neither the immoral, nor idolaters, nor adulterers, nor sexual perverts, nor thieves, nor the greedy, nor drunkards, nor revilers, nor robbers will inherit the kingdom of God. And such were some of you. But you were washed, you were sanctified, you were justified in the name of the Lord Jesus Christ and in the Spirit of our God.
>
> "All things are lawful for me," but not all things are helpful. "All things are lawful for me," but I will not be enslaved by anything. "Food is meant for the stomach and the stomach for food"—and God will destroy both one and the other. The body is not meant for immorality, but for the Lord, and the Lord for the body. And God raised the Lord and will also raise us by His power. Do you not know that your bodies are members of Christ? Shall I therefore take the members of Christ and make them members of a prostitute? Never! Do you not know that he who joins himself to a prostitute becomes one body with her? For, as it is written, "The two shall become one flesh." But he who is united to the Lord becomes one spirit with Him. Shun immorality. Every other sin which a man commits is outside the body; but the immoral man sins against his own body. Do you not know that your body is a temple of the Holy Spirit within you, which you have from God? You are not your own; you were bought with a price. So glorify God in your body. (1 Cor. 6:9-20)[1]

[1]This is the epistle reading for the divine liturgy of the Sunday of the Prodigal Son.

The sexual aspect of human existence, together with all bodily activities, finds its significance when it is wisely and properly integrated into the wholeness of a person's life and behavior. Chastity is the word for this wholeness and wisdom. Chaste persons see reality as it is. They see themselves and others, and indeed all of creation, with a sound and penetrating insight. They are blessed to see even God in the purity of their hearts (Mt. 5:8).

Heaven and earth are filled with God's glory, and the pure in heart see this and delight in it with childlike innocence and enthusiasm. They are the undefiled who walk in the way of the Lord, according to His law, which is indeed His very presence abiding in their hearts. "To the pure," says the apostle Paul, "all things are pure, but to the corrupt and unbelieving nothing is pure; their very minds and consciences are corrupted. They profess to know God, but they deny Him by their deeds; they are detestable, disobedient, unfit for any good deed" (Tit. 1:15-16).

The time of Lent is the time of total purification. It is the season for the conscious striving for the purity of heart by which a person becomes wise and sound, sane and balanced; through which a person comes to see God and to glorify Him by his deeds. It is the time for ceaseless supplication according to the words of David: "Create in me a clean heart, O God, and put a new and right spirit within me. Cast me not away from Thy presence and take not Thy Holy Spirit from me" (Ps. 51:10-12).[2] It is the time for the recovery, indeed the rediscovery, of chastity.

Let us love chastity and flee fornication.
Let us gird up our loins with continence,
    that we may appear in purity before the Savior of
        our souls,
who alone is pure and desires the purification of us all.[3]

[2]These lines are regularly chanted with prostrations at the lenten office of the third hour.
[3]First Wednesday matins.

25

Thrice-Holy Humility

Humility, in the Christian tradition, is called the mother of all virtues. It is the soil out of which grow faith, hope, love and all positive qualities of the spirit.[1] The Psalms proclaim that the Lord leads the humble in what is right and teaches the humble His way. They claim also, with Proverbs and the prophets, that the Lord cares for the humble and gives them His grace. He listens to their prayers and vindicates them before their enemies. He crowns them with victory and clothes them with honor, giving them the whole earth as their inheritance in the unending kingdom which He establishes in the Messiah.

Jesus' teaching about humility is well-known. He says that "every one who exalts himself will be humbled, and he who humbles himself will be exalted" (Lk. 14:11).[2] He commands all to learn from His divine humility and meekness as God's only Son. He connects His teaching about humility with the ability to be childlike.

> And calling to Him a child, He put him in the midst of them, and said, "Truly, I say to you, unless you turn and become like children, you will never enter the kingdom of heaven. Whoever humbles himself like this child, he is the greatest in the kingdom of heaven." (Mt. 18:2-4)

[1]The word humility comes from the Latin *humus*, which means "soil" or "earth." A humble person, therefore, "has his feet on the ground" and is "down to earth."

[2]See also Mt. 23:11-12; Lk. 18:14.

Humility is the most mysterious virtue. It is the most difficult to define and the most elusive to explain. "Those who speak of it in words," says St. Gregory of Sinai, "are like people measuring a bottomless pit." He proceeds, however, in typical fashion, to speak of it himself.

We others, who are blind and guess but a little the meaning of this great light, say: true humility does not say humble words, nor does it assume humble looks, it does not force one to think humbly of oneself, or to abuse oneself in self-belittlement. Although such things are the beginning, the manifestations and the various aspects of humility, humility itself is a grace, given from above.[3]

The saint goes on to explain the various types of humility, the means by which they are attained and the forms through which they are expressed. His final word is that God-given humility is the ability to live by the fact that everything is from God, and through this heartfelt conviction to become "an organ of divine powers" who "performs the inscrutable works of God."[4]

St. John Climacus is more lyrical in his words about "thrice-holy humility." He says that those who have obtained this virtue—the only one which the demons cannot fake— "have won the whole fight."[5] But, again, what is this virtue? How is it defined? How is it explained? He hardly can say.

This subject sets a treasure before us as a touchstone, preserved in earthen vessels, that is to say in our bodies, and it is of a quality that baffles all description. This treasure has one inscription which is incomprehensible because it comes from above, and those who try to explain it with words give themselves great and

---

[3]St. Gregory of Sinai, *Texts on Commandments and Dogmas*, 115. St. Gregory lived in the fourteenth century.

[4]*Texts on Commandments and Dogmas*, 117.

[5]*The Ladder of Divine Ascent*, steps 25:17; 26:49, 126.

endless trouble. And the inscription runs thus: Holy
Humility.[6]

The saint then calls all who are led by the Spirit of God to
gather to investigate the meaning of this precious inscription.
He lists several definitions, and "attentively and soberly"
considering them all, "as a dog gathering crumbs that fall
from the table," he speaks his own word.

> Humility is a nameless grace in the soul, its name
> known only to those who have learned it by experience.
> It is unspeakable wealth, a name and gift from God,
> for it is said: Learn not from an angel, not from man,
> and not from a book, but from Me, that is, from Me
> indwelling, from My illumination and action in you,
> for I am meek and humble in heart and in thought
> and in spirit, and your souls shall find rest from con-
> flicts and relief from arguments.[7]

This is the last and only word. Jesus is humble. And we
learn from him.

> Learn from the Lord, O my soul.
> For your sake He humbled Himself
> even to death on the Cross.
> Exaltation humiliates, but humility exalts!
> Do not become arrogant because of your good deeds.
> Do not justify yourself by judging your neighbor as
>   the self-praising Pharisee did.
> Strive instead in your broken reasoning to cry out
>   with the publican,
> remembering well the great number of your own
>   transgressions:
> "Have mercy on me, O God, have mercy on me!"[8]

The Word humbled Himself to the form of a slave,

[6]Ibid., 25:2.
[7]Ibid., 25:3.
[8]Fourth Thursday vespers.

showing that humility is the path to exaltation.
Every person, then, who humbles himself following
    the example of the Lord
is exalted on high.

You warned us, O Master and Savior,
that You resist the proud but give grace to the humble.
We pray You to send this grace upon us now,
for we have humbled ourselves.

Let us eagerly follow the ways of Jesus the Savior,
learning His humility
in our desire to attain the eternal dwelling of joy
and to find rest in the Land of the Living.[9]

---

[9]Sunday of the Publican and the Pharisee matins. The proverb that "God opposes the proud but gives grace to the humble" is quoted, with commentary, in the letter of James, 4:6-10.

26

Bring Forth Fruit with Patience

When John the Baptist was preparing the people for the coming of Christ, he commanded them to "bear fruits that befit repentance" (Lk. 3:8). Jesus Himself, in preaching repentance, said also that His disciples prove themselves by bringing forth much fruit.

> I am the true vine, and my Father is the vinedresser. Every branch of Mine that bears no fruit, He takes away, and every branch that does bear fruit He prunes, that it may bear more fruit. . . . By this My Father is glorified, that you bear much fruit, and so prove to be My disciples. . . . You did not choose me, but I chose you and appointed you that you should go and bear fruit and that your fruit should abide . . . (Jn. 15:1-2, 8, 16)

Jesus said that His disciples will be known by their fruits (Mt. 7:20). These are the fruits produced by those who are united with Him by the indwelling of the Holy Spirit. They are listed by the apostle Paul in his letter to the Galatians as love, joy, peace, patience, kindness, goodness, faithfulness, gentleness, self-control (5:22). These are the fruits about which the Forerunner spoke when he announced the Lord's coming. And like Jesus in His words about Himself as the true vine, John also foretold that those who fail to produce these fruits would be cut off from God and burned in the fire: "Even now the axe is laid to the root of the trees; every

tree therefore that does not bear good fruit is cut down and
thrown into the fire" (Lk. 3:9; also Jn. 15:1-8).

The lenten season is the time for bearing fruits worthy of
repentance, the fruits of the Spirit. In a sense, this is what
Lent, like life itself, is all about. To produce these holy fruits
is not an easy task. It does not just happen. It is neither
magical nor mechanical. It is a long, hard labor. It requires
much work. And most of all, it takes patience. Jesus made
this point in His explanation of His parable of the sower
when He said that the good earth that receives the seed of
God's Word and brings forth much fruit does so only with
patience: "And as for that in the good soil, they are those
who, hearing the Word, hold it fast in an honest and good
heart, and bring forth fruit with patience" (Lk. 8:15).

In the lenten prayer of St. Ephraim there is a special petition for patience. It is a necessity for the person who expects
to produce spiritual fruits. A garden grows by being tended.
God gives the growth, yet His workers must plow and water
and fertilize and cultivate. This must be done slowly, pain-
fully, with tireless effort and endless patience. Otherwise,
nothing useful will grow. "In your patience," says the Lord
Jesus, "possess ye your souls." Or, in a more modern translation, "By your endurance you will gain your lives" (Lk.
21:19).[1]

The word "patience" means "to endure." It means to bear
and put up with people and things. It means to carry the
burdens of others, and of "the heat of the day." It means to
watch and to wait, not to hurry and to rush. It means literally
to suffer with and to suffer through, in quiet expectation of
the hoped-for result. For only those, says Jesus, who endure
to the end will be saved (Mt. 24:13).

> Be patient, therefore, brethren, until the coming
> of the Lord. Behold, the farmer waits for the precious
> fruit of the earth, being patient over it until it receives
> the early and the late rain. You also be patient. Estab-
> lish your hearts, for the coming of the Lord is at hand.

[1]The first translation is the King James version. The more modern render-
ing is from the Revised Standard text.

Do not grumble, brethren, against one another, that
you may not be judged; behold, the Judge is standing
at the doors. As an example of suffering and patience,
brethren, take the prophets who spoke in the name of
the Lord. Behold, we call those happy who were steadfast. You have heard of the steadfastness of Job, and
you have seen the purpose of the Lord, how the Lord
is compassionate and merciful. (Jas. 5:7-11)

If the lenten spring is to blossom with fruits worthy of repentance, it will do so only with patience.

Come, let us labor in the mystical vineyard,
cultivating there the fruits of repentance.
Let us not spend ourselves in food and drink,
but reap virtues by fasting and prayer.
For these the Master of labor accepts,
giving for them the money with which He redeems
    our souls from the debt of sin,
for He alone is compassionate!

Having passed half the distance of this holy fast,
let us strive rejoicing with patience to its end.
Let us anoint our head with the oil of good deeds,
that we may be worthy to adore the precious passion
    of Christ our God
and to attain to His most honored and holy resurrection.[2]

---

[2]Fourth Sunday matins.

27

As I Have Loved You

If chastity is the heart of every virtue, and humility its mother, and patience its means of attainment, its perfection is certainly love.

Owe no one anything, except to love one another; for he who loves his neighbor has fulfilled the law. The commandments, "You shall not commit adultery, You shall not kill, You shall not steal, You shall not covet," and any other commandment, are summed up in this sentence, "You shall love your neighbor as yourself." Love does no wrong to a neighbor; therefore love is the fulfilling of the law. (Rom. 13:8-10)

Some people think that love is a peculiarly Christian teaching, that it entered the world with Jesus, that it is the special genius of Christianity. This is not true. Jesus Himself quoted the Law of Moses in His teaching.

And one of them, a lawyer, asked Him a question, to test Him. "Teacher, which is the great commandment in the law?" And He said to him, "You shall love the Lord your God with all your heart, and with all your soul, and with all your mind. This is the great and first commandment. And a second is like it, You shall love your neighbor as yourself. On these two commandments depend all the law and the prophets." (Mt. 22:35-40)[1]

[1] The great commandment is found in Deut. 6:5. The second, which is like it, is Lev. 19:18.

The new thing about Jesus' teaching is not the doctrine of
love. It is rather the revelation of love's true meaning and the
"new commandment" that His disciples are to love one another
as He has loved them: "A new commandment I give to you,
that you love one another; even as I have loved you, that you
also love one another. . . . This is My commandment, that
you love one another as I have loved you" (Jn. 13:34; 15:12).
The new thing is the revelation that God Himself is Love.
It is the revelation, scandalous to lovers of power and ridicu-
lous to lovers of wisdom, that God manifests Himself as
Love by dying in human flesh on the Cross for the life of the
world.[2]

> Beloved, let us love one another; for love is of
> God, and he who loves is born of God and knows
> God. He who does not love does not know God; for
> God is love. In this the love of God was made manifest
> among us, that God sent His only Son into the world,
> so that we might live through Him. In this is love,
> not that we loved God but that He loved us and sent
> His Son to be the expiation for our sins. Beloved, if
> God so loved us, we also ought to love one another.
> No man has ever seen God; if we love one another,
> God abides in us and His love is perfected in us. (1
> Jn. 4:7-12)[3]

There is a lot of talk these days about love. There are
lots of slogans and songs. With a little explanation, almost
everyone would agree that love is all around and love is all
you need. And most would also somehow connect love with
the Deity, if there should by chance be one! But how many
would see Love as incarnate in the form of a slave, dying in
the flesh on the Cross? How many would associate Love
with self-denial and obedience, humility and meekness,
slavery and sacrifice? How many would identify Love's absolute fulfillment and most perfect expression as the crucifixion

[2]See 1 Cor. 1:18-2:16.
[3]See also 1 Jn. 4:13-21.

of one's flesh, with its passions and desires, for the well-being of others in imitation of God?[4]

If I speak in tongues of men and of angels, but have not love, I am a noisy gong or a clanging cymbal. And if I have prophetic powers, and understand all mysteries and all knowledge, and if I have all faith, so as to remove mountains, but have not love, I am nothing. If I give away all I have, and if I deliver my body to be burned, but have not love, I gain nothing. Love is patient and kind; love is not jealous or boastful; it is not arrogant or rude. Love does not insist on its own way; it is not irritable or resentful; it does not rejoice at wrong, but rejoices in the right. Love bears all things, believes all things, hopes all things, endures all things. Love never ends; as for prophecies, they will pass away; as for tongues, they will cease; as for knowledge, it will pass away. For our knowledge is imperfect and our prophecy is imperfect; but when the perfect comes, the imperfect will pass away. When I was a child, I spoke like a child, I thought like a child, I reasoned like a child; when I became a man, I gave up childish ways. For now we see in a mirror dimly, but then face to face. Now I know in part; then I shall understand fully, even as I have been fully understood. So faith, hope, love abide, these three; but the greatest of these is love. (1 Cor. 13:1-13)

When considering love, these words of the apostle are all that need saying.

Shine, O Cross of the Lord!
Illumine the hearts of those who adore you
with love inspired by God.
We embrace you, the only hope of the world.
Through you our tears are wiped away,

[4]See Gal. 5:24; 6:14; Rom. 13:14.

and freed from the snares of death
we pass over into everlasting joy.
Reveal Your beauty to us, O Lord, through the Cross.
Help Your servants who ask for mercy in faith.
Bestow upon us the fruits of abstinence.[5]

[5]Third Sunday vespers.

28

By Prayer and Fasting

The lenten spring is consecrated to prayer and fasting.
The practice of abstinence is at the very heart of the effort.
The Church has declared a solemn fast. All are commanded
to join in the action, making their prayers and prostrations
with the "persecution of the stomach."[1]

Jesus Christ fasted and He taught His followers to fast.
His words are familiar:

> And when you fast, do not look dismal, like the
> hypocrites, for they disfigure their faces that their
> fasting may be seen by men. Truly, I say to you, they
> have received their reward. But when you fast, anoint
> your head and wash your face, that your fasting may
> not be seen by men but by your Father who is in
> secret; and your Father who sees in secret will reward
> you. (Mt. 6:16-18)

Jesus did not say, *if* you fast. He said, *when* you fast. Fasting
is part of the spiritual life without which the soul perishes,
suffocated by the flesh and choked by carnal pleasures. A
human being must fast. The effort enlightens the mind,
strengthens the spirit, controls the emotions and tames the
passions. If you do not kill the flesh, the saints tell us, the
flesh kills you.[2] Yet it is not the body as such that is to be

[1] St. John Climacus, *The Ladder of Divine Ascent,* step 5; see above,
"Open to Me the Doors of Repentance," page 40.

[2] An old man in the desert was asked why he was so severe on his body.
He answered simply, "If I don't kill it, it kills me." This saying is repeated
many times in the tradition, lately by St. Seraphim of Sarov.

mortified, it is carnal lusts and desires. "We have not been taught to kill our bodies, but to kill our passions."[3]

The devil is cast out and evil spirits are conquered by prayer and fasting. Not by prayer alone, but by prayer and fasting. When Christ's disciples could not heal a child possessed by a "dumb spirit," the Lord expressed His exasperation with them saying, "O faithless generation, how long am I to be with you? How long am I to bear with you?" Then, after healing the child Himself, He was asked by His disciples why they were powerless to perform this deed. And He said to them, "This kind cannot be driven out by anything but prayer and fasting" (Mk. 9:14-29).[4]

After His baptism in the Jordan by which He identified Himself with sinners, thus revealing Himself as the Suffering Servant and Son of God, Jesus went into the desert to fast. He fasted forty days and forty nights, struggling with Satan. Only then, after His victory over the temptations of the devil, did He begin His messianic work. The apostles also fasted as they accomplished their ministries by the power of the Holy Spirit and by prayer.

> Now in the church at Antioch . . . while they were worshipping the Lord and fasting, the Holy Spirit said, "Set apart for me Barnabas and Saul [i.e., Paul] for the work to which I have called them." Then after fasting and praying they laid their hands on them and sent them off. (Acts 13:1-3)

> When they had preached the gospel in that city [Derbe] and had made many disciples, they returned to Lystra and to Iconium and to Antioch, strengthening the souls of the disciples, exhorting them to continue in the faith, and saying that through many tribulations we must enter the kingdom of God. And when they had appointed elders [presbyters] for them

---

[3]*Sayings of the Desert Fathers*, Poemen, 184; repeated many times, e.g., by Kallistos and Ignatius, *Directions to Hesychasts*, 34.

[4]This is the gospel reading at the liturgy on the Second Sunday of Lent. Some modern versions of the Bible, e.g., RSV, put "and fasting" in a footnote. This reading is that of the Orthodox liturgy.

in every church, with prayer and fasting, they committed them to the Lord in whom they believed. (Acts 14:21-23)

God's work is done by prayer and fasting. There is no other way. Some people deny this, or alter the teaching to suit their own opinions and purposes. They say that God's people need not fast since we are saved by grace and not by works, and that fasting can easily become hypocritical, done merely for show and for the condemnation of others. These people know, like the devil himself, how to quote the scriptures to their advantage. When fasting is mentioned they never fail to produce the proper quotations.

Hear and understand: not what goes into the mouth defiles a man, but what comes out of the mouth, this defiles a man. . . . Are you also still without understanding? Do you not see that whatever goes into the mouth passes into the stomach, and so passes on? But what comes out of the mouth proceeds from the heart, and this defiles a man. For out of the heart come evil thoughts, murder, adultery, fornication, theft, false witness, slander. These are what defile a man; but to eat with unwashed hands does not defile a man. (Mt. 15:10-20)

The point here is not about fasting. Fasting is necessary. But not as an end in itself. It is necessary, like prayer, as a means and a tool. The service of God is the goal, the acquisition of the Holy Spirit and the attainment of His fruits. St. Seraphim of Sarov summed it up in this way:

Prayer, fasting, watching, and all other Christian acts, however good they may be, do not alone constitute the aim of our Christian life, although they serve as the indispensable means of reaching this aim. The true aim of our Christian life is to acquire the Holy Spirit of God.[5]

[5] St. Seraphim of Sarov, "Conversation with N. A. Motovilov."

The church services for the lenten spring make this very point. They warn the faithful not to boast in their fasting, not to flaunt it in public, not to compare themselves with others, not to condemn those who eat. They teach clearly that if one fasts from food while not fasting from sins, one's fasting is in vain. And they constantly remind us, while exhorting us to abstinence, that the devil never eats.

Prayer and fasting are a wonderful weapon
which showed Moses to be the writer of the Law
and Elijah a zealot in sacrifice.
Abiding in them, O faithful, we cry to the Savior:
"Against You have we sinned, have mercy on us!"[6]

Let us keep the Fast not only by refraining from food
but by becoming strangers to all carnal passion,
that we who are enslaved to the tyranny of the flesh
may become worthy to partake of the Lamb, the
        Son of God,
slain by His own will for the salvation of the world,
and to celebrate spiritually the feast of the Savior's
        resurrection from the dead.
So shall we be exalted in the glory of virtues through
        our righteous actions,
Giving joy to the Lord, the Lover of Man.[7]

In vain do you rejoice in not eating, O my soul.
You abstain from food but are not purified from passions.
If you have no desire for improvement, you will be
        despised as a liar in God's eyes.
You will be just like the demons who also never eat.
If you continue in sin, you perform a useless fast.
Therefore remain constant in warfare,
that you may stand before the crucified Savior,
or rather be crucified with Him who dies for your
        sake, saying:
"Remember me, O Lord, when You come in Your
        Kingdom!"[8]

[6]Second Monday matins.
[7]First Tuesday vespers.
[8]Cheesefare Wednesday matins.

29

The Good of His Neighbor

The holy fathers not only fed those who came to them, even on fasting days, but they ate with them as well. Some of the greatest ascetics would even eat and drink more than those whom they were feeding so that their guests would not feel badly, and so that they themselves would not appear to men to be fasting. It was said of St. Macarius the Great and St. Sisoes, two of the very greatest monastic saints, that people were warned that they should not visit them often, and when they did visit for some good purpose, that they should eat and drink very little. For it was the practice of these holy men to fast at least twice as much in secret as they had eaten with their brothers in public. For every piece of bread taken in company, they denied themselves two pieces in private. And for every cup of wine drunk in charity with others, they deprived themselves of two cups of water when alone.[1]

When questioned about their practice, most specifically about why they ate and drank with the brethren, it was usual for the saints to refer to the words of Jesus:

Now John's disciples and the Pharisees were fasting; and people came and said to Him, "Why do John's disciples and the disciples of the Pharisees fast, but Your disciples do not fast?" And Jesus said to them, "Can the wedding guests fast while the bridegroom is with them? As long as they have the bridegroom with them, they cannot fast. The days will come, when the

[1]See *The Sayings of the Desert Fathers*, Macarius the Great, 10: Sisoes, 15.

113

bridegroom is taken away from them, and then they
will fast in that day." (Mk. 2:18-20)[2]

The saints were convinced that every person who came to them
was Christ. They fulfilled literally the teaching that whatever
was done to the least of the brethren was done to the Lord
Himself (Mt. 25:31-46). They believed that every guest was
the Bridegroom, and when the Bridegroom is present one
cannot fast. But when the Bridegroom is taken away, then
the people fast. And they do so in secret (Mt. 6:18).

We Christians nowadays often do the exact opposite of
the saints who ate in public and fasted in secret. We tend to
fast in public and to eat in private. When our churches have
functions during Lent, or when we visit or invite friends
who are fasting, then we fast ourselves. But when we are
alone, we eat. And we generally fabricate good reasons for
ourselves to justify our actions.

The point here is not that Christians as a rule should

[2]This saying of Jesus has a liturgical application in the Orthodox Church
which causes not a little confusion. Great Lent is taken as a season when the
faithful experience the Bridegroom's absence. For this reason the eucharistic
liturgy, with the full anaphora, is not celebrated on weekdays of Great Lent
(with the exception of the feast of the Annunciation). Instead, normally on
Wednesdays and Fridays, the Liturgy of the Presanctified Gifts is served.
This is a solemn lenten vespers with Holy Communion received from the
Gifts consecrated at the previous eucharistic liturgy. On Saturdays and Sundays during Lent, however, because these are holy days at all times, being
the Lord's Sabbath and the Lord's Day, the eucharistic liturgy is celebrated.

Among the misunderstandings which this practice has caused is one relat-
ing to the fact that Canon 55 of Trullo, referring to Apostolic Canon 66,
forbids fasting on Saturday and Sunday during the Great Lent except for
Holy Saturday. The fasting forbidden here is not ascetical fasting and
abstinence. It is the celebration of the Eucharist, Holy Saturday being the
one Saturday during the lenten season when the Eucharist is not served.
Some people take these canons to mean that the ascetical fast is broken on
Saturdays and Sundays during Lent, which cannot be the case since the
Church has the Meatfare and Cheesefare weeks, and then sustains the ascetical
fast straight through the Forty Days of Lent and the following Holy, or
Passion, Week.

Another confusion is that those influenced by Roman Catholicism were
not able to understand the abstention from the eucharistic liturgy on lenten
weekdays since the "mass" was understood primarily, if not exclusively, as a
repetition of Christ's sacrifice on the Cross, which was especially emphasized
during the lenten season. It seemed most strange to them, therefore, and
even impious, to forbid its celebration on weekdays of that season.

consciously break the fast in public. It is not that we should
urge our churches to avoid hypocrisy by serving meat at their
lenten dinners. It is certainly not that we should invite our
pastors to our homes during Lent and then humbly serve them
steak dinners! The point is rather that we should rejoice in
our brothers and sisters at all times. That we should see Christ
the Bridegroom in their person and presence. That we should
celebrate with them as the occasion demands. That we should
always practice hospitality, even if we ourselves are keeping
a fast. That if people are eating and drinking, we should
eat and drink with them, whatever the season, if our actions
will not scandalize them, or if they are not simply tempting us
by their feigned generosity. That we must never appear
"holier than thou." And, most important of all, that we ourselves should fast in secret, hiding our efforts of abstinence
from the eyes of our neighbors.

The apostle Paul makes this very point in another way
and in another context in his letters, sections of which are
read at the divine liturgies during the lenten spring. In his
first letter to the Corinthians, read at the Meatfare Saturday
Eucharist, the apostle writes:

"All things are lawful," but not all things are helpful.
"All things are lawful," but not all things build up.
Let no one seek his own good, but the good of his
neighbor. Eat whatever is sold in the meat market without raising any question on the ground of conscience.
For "the earth is the Lord's, and everything in it." If
one of the unbelievers invites you to dinner and you
are disposed to go, eat whatever is set before you without raising any question on the ground of conscience.
(But if some one says to you, "This has been offered
in sacrifice," then out of consideration for the man who
informed you, and for conscience' sake—I mean his
conscience, not yours—do not eat it.) (1 Cor. 10:23-
29)[3]

In his letter to the Romans St. Paul makes the same point.

[3]See also the epistle reading for Meatfare Sunday, 1 Cor. 8:8-9:2.

This passage from his letter is read at the Cheesefare Saturday liturgy.

> Let us then pursue what makes for peace and for mutual upbuilding. Do not, for the sake of food, destroy the work of God. Everything is indeed clean, but it is wrong for any one to make others fall by what he eats; it is right not to eat meat or drink wine or do anything that makes your brother stumble. The faith that you have, keep between yourself and God; happy is he who has no reason to judge himself for what he approves. But he who has doubts is condemned, if he eats, because he does not act from faith; for whatever does not proceed from faith is sin. We who are strong ought to bear with the failings of the weak, and not to please ourselves; let each of us please his neighbor for his good, to edify him. (Rom. 14:19-15:2)[4]

The case presented here by the apostle is that a Christian's eating may at times lead his neighbor into temptation, scandal and sin. In such cases, the Christian should not eat. The same holy fathers, for example, who would eat with their guests who came in good will would refuse to eat with others who visited them. When asked about their behavior, the saints would reply that these others came only to see if and what they would eat, so with such people they offered nothing and abstained themselves.[5]

The teaching here is delicate and subtle. But it should be clear to those willing to understand in purity of heart. The good of one's neighbor is the only absolute law. The expression of love is the rule in every instance. Sometimes we are called to eat with our neighbors in love. And sometimes the same love demands, for their sake and not ours, that we

---

[4]See also the epistle reading for Cheesefare Sunday, Rom. 13:11-14:4.

[5]The holy fathers followed the same practice in regard to talk and silence. They would talk at any time, at any length, even during the liturgy, with those who sought such conversation for their salvation. But they would not speak at all to those who came only to hear what they would say, with no intention of putting the words into practice. See, e.g., *The Ladder of Divine Ascent*, step 26:69.

abstain. The apostle Paul summarizes his own inspired instructions in these words: "So, whether you eat or drink, or
whatever you do, do all to the glory of God. Give no offense
to Jews or to Greeks or to the church of God, just as I try to
please all men in everything I do, not seeking my own advantage, but that of many, that they may be saved" (1 Cor.
10:31-33).

> Let us hasten to cleanse the pollution of our sins
> through fasting, charity and love for the poor,
> that we may enter the wedding feast of the
>   Bridegroom Christ,
> Who grants us great mercy.[6]

[6]Cheesefare Monday vespers.

30

Why Have We Fasted?

"Why have we fasted, and Thou seest it not? Why have we humbled ourselves, and Thou takest no knowledge of it?" (Is. 58:3). These questions of God's people recorded by the prophet Isaiah are questions which we still ask today. And the answer which the Lord provides is still the same:

"Why have we fasted, and Thou seest it not? Why have we humbled ourselves, and Thou takest no knowledge of it?"

Behold, in the day of your fast you seek your own pleasure, and oppress all your workers. Behold, you fast only to quarrel and to fight and to hit with wicked fist. Fasting like yours this day will not make your voice to be heard on high. Is such the fast that I choose, a day for a man to humble himself? Is it to bow down his head like a rush, and to spread sackcloth and ashes under him? Will you call this a fast, and a day acceptable to the Lord? (Is. 58:3-5)

The Lord's teaching is clear. The people fast and go through ritual acts of repentance without a real and genuine turning to God. They humble themselves externally, abstaining from foods, making prostrations, spreading sackcloth and ashes, without keeping the commandments of the Lord. Under such conditions their prayers will not be heard, and their ritual offerings will not be received. Their splendid liturgies will be offensive to God, and their incense will be an abomination in His sight.

What to Me is the multitude of your sacrifices? . . .
Bring no more vain offerings; incense is an abomination
to Me. New moon and sabbath and the calling of
solemn assemblies—I cannot endure iniquity and
solemn assembly. Your new moons and your appointed
feasts my soul hates; they have become a burden to
Me, I am weary of bearing them. When you spread
forth your hands, I will hide My eyes from you; even
though you make many prayers, I will not listen; your
hands are full of blood. (Is. 1:11-15)

These words of the Lord through Isaiah are found in all the
prophetic proclamations. Jeremiah is even commanded by the
Lord to cease praying for the people even though they themselves fast and pray, because their deeds are vile.

Therefore do not pray for this people, or lift up a
cry or prayer on their behalf, for I will not listen when
they call to me in the time of their trouble. What right
has my beloved in my house, when she has done vile
deeds? (Jer. 11:14-15)

The Lord said to me: "Do not pray for the welfare
of this people. Though they fast, I will not hear their
cry, and though they offer burnt offering and cereal
offering, I will not accept them; but I will consume
them by the sword, by famine, and by pestilence."
(Jer. 14:11-12)

What must be done is simple and clear. God's people must
keep His commandments. Their prayers and fasting, their
temple worship and sacrifice, their offerings and incense must
be directed to this end. If it is not, it not only is accomplished
in vain. It is done unto condemnation and judgment.[1]

---

[1]The very act of Holy Communion can be for condemnation when it is
received as a mere ritual, without sincere repentance and the struggle to keep
God's commandments. So the faithful pray before the Eucharist: "May the
communion of Your Holy Mysteries be neither to my judgment nor to my
condemnation, O Lord, but to the healing of soul and body."

Is not this the fast that I choose: to loose the bonds of wickedness, to undo the thongs of the yoke, to let the oppressed go free, and to break every yoke? Is it not to share your bread with the hungry, and bring the homeless poor into your house; when you see the naked, to cover him, and not to hide yourself from your own flesh? Then shall your light break forth like the dawn, and your healing shall spring up speedily; your righteousness shall go before you, the glory of the Lord shall be your rear guard. Then you shall call, and the Lord will answer; you shall cry, and He will say, Here I am.

If you take away from the midst of you the yoke, the pointing of the finger, and speaking wickedness, if you pour yourself out for the hungry and satisfy the desire of the afflicted, then shall your light rise in the darkness and your gloom be as the noonday. And the Lord will guide you continually, and satisfy your desire with good things, and make your bones strong; and you shall be like a watered garden, like a spring of water, whose waters fail not. And your ancient ruins shall be rebuilt; you shall raise up the foundations of many generations; you shall be called the repairer of the breach, the restorer of streets to dwell in. (Is. 58:6-12)

Not those who say "Lord, Lord" will enter God's kingdom, Jesus teaches, but those who actually do the will of His Father (Mt. 7:21). The lenten services, as may be expected, repeat this point constantly.

Now the time of the holy fast has come.
Let us begin it with a return to good actions,
for it is written:
In quarrels and fighting you shall not fast![2]

While fasting physically, O people,
let us also fast spiritually.

[2]First Monday matins.

Let us loose every knot of iniquity;
let us tear up every righteous bond;
let us distribute bread to the hungry
and welcome the homeless into our homes,
that we may receive great mercy from Christ our God![3]

[3]First Wednesday vespers.

31

St. John Chrysostom on Fasting

The Christian teaching about fasting is well summed up by St. John Chrysostom.

> When the fast makes its appearance, like a kind of spiritual summer, let us as soldiers burnish our weapons, and as harvesters sharpen our sickles, and as sailors order our thoughts against the waves of extravagant desires, and as travellers set out on the journey towards heaven, and as wrestlers strip for the contest. For the believer is at once a harvester and a sailor and a soldier, a wrestler and a traveller. . . .

> Sharpen your sword and your sickle which has been blunted by gluttony—sharpen it by fasting. Lay hold of the pathway which leads towards heaven, rugged and narrow as it is. Lay hold of it, and journey on.

> I speak not of such a fast as most persons keep, but of real fasting; not merely abstinence from meats, but from sins as well. For the nature of a fast is such that it does not suffice to deliver those who practice it unless it is done according to a suitable law. So that when we have gone through the labor of fasting we do not lose the crown of fasting, we must understand how and in what manner it is necessary to conduct the business since the Pharisee also fasted, but afterward went away empty and destitute of the fruit of fasting. The Publican did not fast, and yet he was accepted in prefer-

ence to him who had fasted in order that you may learn that fasting is unprofitable unless all other duties accompany it.

Fasting is a medicine. But like all medicines, though it be very profitable to the person who knows how to use it, it frequently becomes useless (and even harmful) in the hands of him who is unskillful in its use.

I have said these things not that we may disparage fasting, but that we may honor fasting. For the honor of fasting consists not in abstinence from food, but in withdrawing from sinful practices, since he who limits his fasting only to abstinence from meats is one who especially disparages fasting.

Do you fast? Give me proof of it by your works. By what kind of works? If you see a poor man, take pity on him. If you see an enemy, be reconciled with him. If you see a friend gaining honor, do not be jealous of him. If you see a beautiful woman, pass her by. And let not only the mouth fast, but also the eye and the ear and the feet and the hands and all members of your bodies.

Let the hands fast by being pure from plundering and avarice. Let the feet fast by ceasing from running to unlawful spectacles. Let the eyes fast, being taught never to fix themselves rudely on handsome faces, or to busy themselves with strange beauties. For looking is the food of the eyes, but if it be such as is unlawful or forbidden, it mars the fast and upsets the whole safety of the soul. But if it be lawful and safe, it adorns fasting. For it would be among things most absurd to abstain from lawful food because of the fast, but with the eyes to touch even what is forbidden! Do you not eat meat? Feed not upon lasciviousness by means of your eyes! Let the ear fast also. The fasting of the ear consists in refusing to receive evil speakings and calumnies. It is written, "You shall not receive a false report" (Ex. 23:1, LXX).

Let the mouth also fast from disgraceful speeches and railings. For what does it profit if we abstain from fish and fowl and yet bite and devour the brothers and sisters. The evil speaker eats the flesh of his brother and bites the body of his neighbor. Because of this Paul utters the fearful saying, "If you bite and devour one another take heed that you are not consumed by one another" (Gal. 5:15). You have not fixed your teeth in his flesh, but you have fixed your slander in his soul and inflicted the wound of evil suspicion, and you have harmed in a thousand ways yourself and him and many others, for in slandering your neighbor you have made him who listens to the slander worse, for should he be a wicked person, he becomes more careless when he finds a partner in his wickedness. And should he be a just person, he is tempted to arrogance and gets puffed up, being led on by the sin of others to imagining great things concerning himself. Besides this, you have struck at the common welfare of the Church herself, for all those who hear you will not only accuse the supposed sinner, but the entire Christian community. . . .

And so I desire to fix three precepts in your mind so that you may accomplish them during the fast: to speak ill of no one, to hold no one for an enemy, and to expel from your mouth altogether the evil habit of swearing.

For if, as the harvester in the fields comes to the end of his labors little by little, so we too if we make this rule for ourselves and in any manner come to the correct practice of these three precepts during the present Lent and commit them to the safe custody of good habit, we shall proceed with greater ease to the rest, and by this means attain to the summit of spiritual wisdom. And we shall reap the harvest of a favorable hope in this life, and in the life to come we shall stand before Christ with great confidence and enjoy those unspeakable blessings of which, God grant, we may all be found worthy through the grace of Jesus Christ our Lord, with whom be glory to the Father and to the Holy Spirit unto ages of ages. Amen.[1]

Come, O faithful!
Let us accomplish the works of God in light.
Let us walk honestly as in the day.
Let us rid ourselves of unjust accusations against
     our neighbors,
that we may place no stumbling block in their way.
Let us lay aside all pleasures of the flesh,
that we may increase gifts to our souls.
Let us give bread to the needy.
Let us draw near to Christ in repentance and say:
"O our God, have mercy on us!"[2]

---

[1]St. John Chrysostom, *Concerning the Statues,* homily 3.
[2]First Friday vespers.

32

When You Give Alms

In His sermon on the mount Jesus not only gives instructions about prayer and fasting, He gives commandments about almsgiving as well. Indeed, in the sermon, this part comes first.

> . . . when you give alms, sound no trumpet before you, as the hypocrites do in the synagogues and in the streets, that they may be praised by men. Truly, I say to you, they have received their reward. But when you give alms, do not let your left hand know what your right hand is doing, so that your alms may be in secret; and your Father who sees in secret will reward you. (Mt. 6:2-4)

Jesus, once again, did not say, *if* you give alms. He said, *when* you give alms. In this, as in all of His teachings, He confirms the commandments of God's law in the old covenant. (See Ex. 22:21-27; Lev. 25:35-37.)

> He who despises his neighbor is a sinner,
>   but happy is he who is kind to the poor. . . .
> He who oppresses a poor man insults his Maker,
>   but he who is kind to the needy honors Him.
>   (Prov. 14:21, 31)

The apostles of Christ magnified the Master's teaching about the need to help the needy. They insisted that human perfection consists in giving to the poor and following Christ. They taught, with Jesus, that the measure one gives is the measure one gets. They were convinced that the greatest imitation of God is to give everything without asking anything in return. And when such perfection could not be literally accomplished, the commandment to share one's possessions, not from one's abundance but out of one's needs, was considered binding on all.[1]

> Now the company of those who believed were of one heart and soul, and no one said that any of the things which he possessed was his own, but they had everything in common. And with great power the apostles gave their testimony to the resurrection of the Lord Jesus, and great grace was upon them all. There was not a needy person among them, for as many as were possessors of lands or houses sold them, and brought the proceeds of what was sold and laid it at the apostles' feet; and distribution was made to each as any had need. (Acts 4:32-35)

According to the scriptures, the giving of one's possessions to satisfy the needs of others is the most concrete expression of faith and of love. A person who claims to believe in God but does not help the needy has no living faith.

> What does it profit, my brethren, if a man says he has faith but has not works? Can his faith save him? If a brother or sister is ill-clad and in lack of daily food, and one of you says to them, "Go in peace, be warmed and filled," without giving them the things needed for the body, what does it profit? So faith by itself, if it has no works, is dead. (Jas. 2:14-17)

And a person who claims to love God and his neighbors, but fails to express his love in acts of generosity, is a self-deceived liar.

> By this we know love, that He laid down His life for

[1]See Mk. 4:24; Mt. 7:2; Lk. 6:32-38, 18:22, 21:1-4.

us; and we ought to lay down our lives for the brethren. But if any one has the world's goods and sees his
brother in need, yet closes his heart against him, how
does God's love abide in him? Little children, let us
not love in word or speech but in deed and in truth.
(1 Jn. 3:16-18)

Among the saints no one is more insistent on the necessity
of almsgiving than St. John Chrysostom. He identifies alms
with the oil in the lamps of the virgins in Christ's parable.
Without this oil of almsgiving, our lamps are not lit and we
cannot enter into the bridal chamber of Christ. He calls
generosity the treasury of the Church through which we are
made godlike. For those who can give alms but do not, there
is no salvation. Feed the needy now, Chrysostom proclaims,
or be ready forever to feed the fires of hell.[2]

Do you see that the failure to give alms is enough to
cast a person into hell-fire? For where will he avail
who does not give alms? Do you fast every day? So
also did those foolish virgins, but it availed them
nothing. Do you pray? So did they. What of it? Prayer
without almsgiving is unfruitful. Without that all
things are unclean and unprofitable. The better part of
virtue is destroyed. "He who does not love his brother," it is said, "does not know God" (1 John 4:8).
And how do you love him, when you do not even give
him these things which are worthless and passing. . . .
Here we can resemble God, in showing mercy and
generosity. When we have not these qualities, we are
devoid of all good.[3]

For almsgiving is the mother of love, of that love
which is characteristic of Christianity, which is greater
than all miracles, by which the disciples of Christ are
manifested.[4]

[2]St. John Chrysostom, *On Philippians*, 2.
[3]*On II Timothy*, 6.
[4]*On Titus*, 6.

Woe to him, it is said, who does not give alms. And
if this was the case under the Old Covenant, much
more is it under the New. . . . For what did they of
old not do? They gave tithes, and tithes upon tithes,
for orphans and widows and strangers. Recently someone said to me of a Christian: "Why, such a person
gives tithes!" What a disgrace this expression implies!
What was not a matter of wonder with the Jews has
come to be so in the case of Christians! If there was
danger then in omitting tithes, think how great it must
be now![5]

For what is required is that we give, not much or little,
but not less than is in our power. Think about the
widow . . . who gave her whole living. But you in the
midst of your plenty are more stingy than she. Let us
not be careless for our own salvation, but apply ourselves to almsgiving. For nothing is better than this,
as the time to come will tell. . . .[6]

St. Basil the Great is no less insistent on this subject than
St. John. "He who takes another's clothing is called a thief,"
he writes, "but he who fails to clothe the naked, if he could,
deserves the very same name. The grain in your barns belongs
to the hungry. The coat in your closet belongs to the naked.
The shoes rotting in your basement belong to the barefoot.
The silver hidden in boxes belongs to the needy. You sin
against all those whom you are able to help, but fail to do
so."[7]

These teachings of the saints are those of Christ and the
Church.

Come, let us purify our souls with alms and mercy
    to the poor,
not blowing the trumpet or publishing what we do in
    charity,

[5] *On Ephesians*, 4.
[6] *On Colossians*, 1.
[7] St. Basil the Great, *Against the Rich*, 6. See also Chrysostom, *On Lazarus*, 2.

lest our left hand know what our right hand has done,
and vainglory steal from us the fruit of our alms.
But let us plead in secret with the One who knows
        all secrets:
"Father, forgive us our wrongs,
for You are the only Lover of Man!"[8]

If we set our hands to doing good,
the effort of Lent will be a time of repentance for us,
a means to eternal life.
For nothing saves so much as giving to those in need.
Alms inspired by fasting delivers a person from death.
Let us embrace the giving of alms,
for it has no equal [in the spiritual life].
It is sufficient to save our souls.[9]

[8]First Sunday vespers.
[9]Second Thursday matins.

33

You Did It Unto Me

Like life itself, of which it is the liturgical image, the lenten season is a preparation for God's final judgment. Its entire effort is directed, as the Church prays daily, to a "good defense before the dread judgment seat of Christ." From the beginning of the lenten spring until its very end, the faithful live and work in view of this judgment, the conditions of which are well known: Jesus reveals them in His famous parable which is read at the liturgy of Meatfare Sunday before Great Lent begins, and again during the services of Holy Week, when the Forty Days are over.

When the Son of Man comes in His glory, and all the angels with Him, then He will sit on His glorious throne. Before Him will be gathered all the nations, and He will separate them one from another as a shepherd separates the sheep from the goats, and He will place the sheep at His right hand, but the goats at the left. Then the King will say to those at His right hand, "Come, O blessed of My Father, inherit the kingdom prepared for you from the foundation of the world; for I was hungry and you gave Me food, I was thirsty and you gave Me drink, I was a stranger and you welcomed Me, I was naked and you clothed Me, I was sick and you visited Me, I was in prison and you came to Me." Then the righteous will answer Him, "Lord, when did we see Thee hungry and feed Thee, or thirsty and give Thee drink? And when did we see Thee a stranger and welcome Thee, or naked

and clothe Thee? And when did we see Thee sick or
in prison and visit Thee?" And the King will answer
them, "Truly, I say to you, as you did it to one of the
least of these My brethren, you did it to Me."

Then He will say to those at His left hand, "Depart
from Me, you cursed, into the eternal fire prepared
for the devil and his angels; for I was hungry and you
gave Me no food, I was thirsty and you gave Me no
drink, I was a stranger and you did not welcome Me,
naked and you did not clothe Me, sick and in prison
and you did not visit Me." Then they also will answer, "Lord, when did we see Thee hungry or thirsty
or a stranger or naked or sick or in prison, and did not
minister to Thee?" Then He will answer them, "Truly,
I say to you, as you did it not to one of the least of
these, you did it not to Me." And they will go away
into eternal punishment, but the righteous into eternal
life. (Mt. 25:31-46)

We must return to this parable again and again. We must
contemplate it daily. It should never leave our attention. It
should be engraved in our minds and embedded in our hearts.
All our efforts of prayer and fasting, especially during Lent,
are directed to its fulfillment. Our eternal life depends on its
accomplishment.

The parable speaks about specific acts: feeding the hungry,
giving drink to the thirsty, welcoming the stranger, clothing
the naked, visiting the sick and imprisoned. Jesus Christ Himself is the object of these acts. Being Himself the Bread of
Life, He hungers in order to be with the hungry and to feed
them with His own Body and Blood. He who pours forth the
Living Water Himself thirsts on the cross that through His
thirst He may assuage the thirst of His people through the
outpouring of His Spirit. Alien and unwelcome in His very
own world, He identifies with the outcast in order to bring
them home to the house of His Father. Naked in the manger,
naked in the River Jordan, naked upon the Cross, naked in
the tomb, He is naked with all the naked that He might clothe
them with Himself in the robes of righteousness and the

garments of salvation. Wounded for our transgressions, a criminal before Pilate, He takes our wounds and infirmities upon Himself and heals them all in His own body and soul upon the Tree of the Cross, forgiving our sins. Our treatment of the hungry, thirsty, alien, naked, sick and imprisoned, therefore, is our treatment of Christ Himself. He is the "least of the brethren" for us.

St. Simeon the New Theologian, than whom none is more mystical in Orthodox tradition, identified spiritual perfection with the fulfillment of Jesus' parable of the last judgment. He saw in this parable not simply the commandment to perform certain specific acts of charity. He saw in it the entire meaning of the spiritual life.

> A person is not saved by having once shown mercy to someone, although if he scorns someone but once he deserves eternal fire. For "I was hungry," and "I was thirsty" was said not just of one occasion, not of one day, but of the whole of life. In the same way "you gave me food," "you gave me drink," "you clothed me" and so on does not indicate one incident, but *a constant attitude to everyone*.

> Our Lord was pleased to assume the likeness of every poor man and compared Himself to every poor man in order that no man who believes in Him should exalt himself over his brother, but, seeing the Lord in his brother, should consider himself less and worse than his brother, just as he is less than his Creator. And he should take the poor man in and honor him, and be ready to exhaust all his means in helping him, just as our Lord Jesus Christ exhausted His blood for our salvation.

> It is clear . . . that the Lord accepts and takes everything done for our poor neighbors as done for Himself. And His words "You did it to me," are not limited only to those to whom we were unkind, or those whom we wronged, or those whose possessions we have taken,

or to whom we have done harm, but include also
those whom we have disdained or neglected. This latter
alone is sufficient for our condemnation for, in disdain-
ing anyone, we disdain Christ Himself.

All this may appear too hard to people and they may
think it right to say to themselves: "Who can strictly
follow all this, satisfying and feeding everyone and
leaving no one unsatisfied?" Let them listen to Paul
who says clearly: "For the love of Christ controls us,
because we are convinced that one has died for all;
therefore all have died. And he died for all, that those
who live might live no longer for themselves but for
him who, for their sake, died and was raised."[1]

The Russian St. Seraphim, in so many ways akin to St.
Simeon in his mystical gifts, his communion with the Uncreated Light, his stress that the aim of the Christian life is
the acquisition of the Holy Spirit, sums up his teaching also
by reference to this parable of Christ. "So be it, God-loving
one," he says to Motovilov in conclusion to their famous
conversation in the snow. "Whatever you ask of the Lord
God, you shall receive, provided it is for the glory of God
and the good of your neighbor, because that which profits
our neighbor He adds all to His glory, for He says: 'As you
did it to one of the least of these my brethren, you did it to
me.' "

The kingdom of God is not food and drink;
it is truth and abstinence in righteousness.
So the rich shall not enter into it,
but only those who place gifts in the hands of the poor.
This too is the teaching of David the prophet:
"The righteous man is merciful all the day.
He delights in the Lord and walks in the light.

[1]St. Simeon the New Theologian, *Practical and Theological Precepts*, 123-
131. St. Simeon lived in the eleventh century near Constantinople. He is
called the "new theologian" after St. Gregory of Nazianzus because of his
mystical theology, much of which is expressed, like St. Gregory's, in poetic
form.

He shall not stumble or fall."
This is written for our instruction,
that we might fulfill the Fast with good works,
and the Lord shall reward us.[2]

Judge of all, my God and Lord,
may I hear Your words of blessing on that day.
May I see Your mighty light.
May I look upon Your mansions.
May I behold Your glory,
and rejoice forever.[3]

[2]Fifth Sunday matins.
[3]Meatfare Sunday matins.

34

Our Brother is Our Life

The purpose of all prayer and fasting, of all liturgy and sacraments, of all spiritual exercises and ascetic practices, is to come to know and love God in all people and things, especially our enemies and the "least of the brethren." This is the purpose of the lenten spring and of life itself. It is the highest and greatest mystery, the deepest and most profound truth: God is seen, known and loved in everyone and everything. For the only-begotten Son of God has come to earth in creaturely form in order to unite all things in Himself, things in heaven and things on earth (Eph. 1:10). He has come to identify Himself with everyone and everything, especially the sinful, the wayward and the lost. He, being our God and Creator, has become our brother and our slave. And so in Him we encounter everyone and everything. And in everyone and everything we encounter Him.

The elder Silouan (Silvanus), a monk of Mount Athos who died in 1938, came to know this deepest mystery and most profound truth through his own spiritual experience. He bore witness to it in his writings, which are perfect reading for the lenten season.

These forty years, ever since the Lord through the Holy Spirit gave me to know the love of God, have I grieved over God's people.

O brethren, there is nothing better than the love of God when the Lord fires the soul with love for God and our fellow-man.

The man who knows the delight of the love of God—
when the soul, warmed by grace, loves both God and
her brother—knows in part that "the kingdom of God
is within us." Blessed is the soul that loves her brother,
for *our brother is our life.*

Forty years have gone by since the grace of the Holy
Spirit taught me to love mankind and every created
thing. . . .

If we wish to love God we must observe all that the
Lord commanded in the Gospels. Our hearts must
brim with compassion and not only feel love for fellow-
men but pity for every creature—for every thing created
by God.

The Lord wants us to love our fellow-man; and if you
reflect that the Lord loves him, that is a sign of the
Lord's love in you. And if you consider how greatly
the Lord loves His creature, and you yourself have
compassion on all creation, and love your enemies,
counting yourself the vilest of men, this is a sign of
abundant grace of the Holy Spirit in you.

The man who has the Holy Spirit within him, in however slight a degree, sorrows day and night for all
mankind. His heart is filled with pity for all of God's
creatures, and more especially for those who do not
know God or who resist Him. . . . For them, more
than for himself, he prays night and day, that all may
repent and know the Lord.

I beseech you, put this to the test. When a man affronts
you or brings dishonor on your head, or takes what is
yours, or persecutes the Church, pray to the Lord
and say: "O Lord, we are all Thy creatures. Have pity
on Thy servants and turn their hearts to repentance,"
and you will be aware of grace in your soul. To begin
with, constrain your heart to love her enemies, and

the Lord, seeing your good will, will help you in all
things, and experience itself will show you the way.
But the person who thinks with malice on his enemies
has not God's love within him and does not know God.

"The enemy persecutes our Holy Church," you may say,
"am I then to love him?" But my answer is this: "Your
poor soul has not come to know God, and how greatly
He loves us, and how longingly He looks for all people
to repent and be saved. The Lord is love, and He sent
the Holy Spirit on earth, who teaches the soul to love
her enemies and pray for them that they too may find
salvation. That is true love."[1]

Commenting on the apostle's teaching in the first letter
to Timothy, that Christians ought always to offer supplications, prayers, intercessions and thanksgiving for all people
since God our Savior "desires all men to be saved and to come
to the knowledge of the truth" (1 Tim. 2:1-4), St. John
Chrysostom, more than fifteen hundred years before the elder
Silouan, gives the same teaching. "Imitate God!" he writes.
"If He wills that all men should be saved, there is reason
that one should pray for all. If He wills that all should be
saved, you should be willing too. And if you wish it, pray
for it; for wishes lead to prayers. . . . Fear not therefore to
pray for the heathen, for God Himself wills it. But fear only
to pray against any, for He does not will that. And if you
pray for the heathen, you ought also to pray for heretics, for
we are to pray for all people and to persecute none. And this
is so for another reason as well. Since we are all partakers of
the same nature, God commands and accepts our benevolence
and affection towards one another."

Chrysostom bases his exhortation on the doctrine of the
incarnation of the Son of God in human flesh, through which
He becomes our brother and is identified with all people,
including the heathen. For, the apostle writes, He "gave
Himself as a ransom for all. . . ." (1 Tim. 2:6). "And what

[1]*Wisdom from Mount Athos*, pp. 29-36.

does ransom mean?" Chrysostom asks. And he answers himself:

> God was about to punish them, but He forbore to do it. They were about to perish, but instead He gave His own Son. . . . What no one would do for his friends, relatives or children, that the Lord does for His servants. And not even as a Lord for servants, but as God for men, and undeserving men at that! For what men would not do for their fellow-men, that God has done for us. Yet after such a display of love toward us, we still hold back, and are not in earnest in our love for Christ. He has sacrificed Himself for us, and yet for Him we make no sacrifice.[2]

St. Anthony the Great sums up this entire teaching in a few short sentences. "Our life and our death is with our neighbor," he writes. "If we gain our brother, we have gained God. But if we scandalize our brother, we have sinned against Christ."[3] And, as we have seen, the elder Silouan says it all in five brief words: "Our brother is our life."

> Daniel the prophet, greatly beloved,
> when he saw the power of God cried out:
> "The court sat in judgment and the books were opened!"
> Consider well, O my soul.
> Do you fast? Then despise not your brother.
> Do you abstain from food? Then condemn not your
>   neighbor,
> lest you burn as wax in the fire.
> May Christ lead you without stumbling into
>   His kingdom.[4]

---

[2]St. John Chrysostom, *On Timothy*, homily 7.
[3]*The Sayings of the Desert Fathers*, St. Anthony, 9.
[4]Meatfare Sunday vespers.

35

Tempted as We Are, Yet Without Sin

The identification of the Son of God with us sinners finds its completion upon the Cross. The apostle Paul, as usual, says it clearly and bluntly. We were cursed because of our rebellion. So "Christ redeemed us from the curse of the law, having become a curse for us—for it is written, 'Cursed be every one who hangs on a tree'" (Gal. 3:13, quoting Deut. 21:23). We are sinful because of our disobedience. So for our sake God made His very own Son "to be sin who knew no sin, so that in Him we might become the righteousness of God" (2 Cor. 5:21). Jesus Christ is a curse for us, and sin itself, by taking on our sins through His death on the Cross.

The Cross is the goal of the lenten spring. We fast and pray and worship and struggle to be made worthy to behold the passion of the Lord, and His holy resurrection. The lenten services repeat this over and again. The end is the Cross. And therefore, as is typical of Orthodox liturgy, the Cross is also placed directly in the middle of the season, with the entire third week of Lent being completely devoted to its veneration and contemplation.

The epistle reading for the Sunday Eucharist, at whose vigil the decorated Cross is solemnly placed in the center of the church, is taken, as are all lenten epistle readings, from the letter to the Hebrews.

Since then we have a great high priest who has passed through the heavens, Jesus, the Son of God, let us hold fast our confession. For we have not a high priest who is unable to sympathize with our weaknesses, but one

who in every respect has been tempted as we are, yet
without sinning. Let us then with confidence draw
near to the throne of grace, that we may receive mercy
and find grace to help in time of need. For every high
priest chosen from among men is appointed to act on
behalf of men in relation to God, to offer gifts and
sacrifices for sins. He can deal gently with the ignorant
and wayward, since he himself is beset with weakness.
Because of this he is bound to offer sacrifice for his
own sins as well as for those of the people. And one
does not take the honor upon himself, but he is called
by God, just as Aaron was. So also Christ did not exalt
Himself to be made a high priest, but was appointed
by Him who said to Him, "Thou art My Son, today I
have begotten Thee"; as He says also in another place,
"Thou art a priest for ever, after the order of Mel-
chizedek." (Heb. 4:14-5:6)

The author of this letter makes it clear that Jesus "in the
days of His flesh" really and truly suffered. He offered up
"prayers and supplications with loud cries and tears." We
see this in Gethsemane and on Golgotha. And, say the holy
scriptures, God's own Son "learned obedience through what
He suffered; and being made perfect, He became the source
of eternal salvation to all who obey Him" (Heb. 5:7-9).

If we would truly grasp what is being said here, it would,
as the saying goes, blow our minds! We simply could not
handle it. It would be too much for us to bear. God's own
Son has come to sympathize (which means literally to *suffer
with*) our weakness. God's own Son who, as this epistle says,
is the One through whom God created the world, being the
radiance of God's glory and the exact image of God's person,
the One who upholds the universe by the word of His power
(see Heb. 1:1-3),[1] He, and no other, has come to be "tempted

---

[1]In these lines taken from Hebrews, the RSV translates nouns by verbs.
The Son is not He who "reflects the glory of God" and who "bears the very
stamp of His nature." He is rather Himself the *radiance* or *reflection* of
God's glory, the One who Himself is the *very stamp* or *exact image* of the
Father's *nature* or *person*. (In Greek this last sentence says that the Son is
the *kharakter* of the Father's *hypostasis*.)

as we are tempted, yet without sin" so that through His temptations and tribulations, through His weaknesses and wounds, we could be healed, strengthened, purified and saved.

The entire lenten spring exists for us to become aware of Christ's voluntary passion for our sake. The season specifically exists for us to strive to penetrate this mystery, and to be penetrated by it. It exists for us to be made perfect through our obedience to Him and our suffering in Him, with Him and for Him, the Source of our salvation. It exists for us to be enabled to draw near to God's throne of grace with confidence, that we may receive mercy and find grace to help in all times of need within the wayward world in which we live.

> Wishing to restore all people to life,
> You accepted crucifixion, O Christ our God!
> Burning with boundless love for man,
> You took the quill of the Cross in Your hands.
> Dipping it in the ink of royal crimson,
> You signed our release with Your hands stained
>   with blood.
> Though temptations assault us, may we never again
>   forsake You.
> Have mercy on Your despairing people, O
>   long-suffering Master.
> Arise and fight our enemies in Your almighty power.[2]

---

[2]Third Sunday vespers.

36

Made Like His Brethren in Every Respect

The lenten spring is the time for contemplating the deepest mysteries of human existence, the most profound truths concerning God and man. These mysteries and truths are summed up and fulfilled in Christ on the Tree of the Cross. Here is where the God who is Love reveals Himself in the Son of His Love, crucified in love for the sake of His beloved. Here is where divine perfection is fully revealed, and human perfection is fully realized in the one person of Jesus Christ who is truly both God and man.

> But we see Jesus, who for a little while was made lower than the angels, crowned with glory and honor because of the suffering of death, so that by the grace of God He might taste death for every one. For it was fitting that He, for whom and by whom all things exist, in bringing many sons to glory, should make the pioneer of their salvation perfect through suffering. (Heb. 2:9-10)

Jesus the Messiah, a real human being just as we all are except for our sins, was tempted in His humanity. He had freely to submit His human will to the will of His Father. The devil made every effort to divert Jesus from this awesome achievement. Immediately after His baptism, through which He revealed Himself as the Lamb of God who takes upon Himself the sins of the world, Jesus was led into the desert "to be tempted by the devil" (Mt. 4:1). He fasted and prayed for forty days and nights. And Satan came to Him to tempt

Him to follow the ways of the world. He came to entice Him to try to be the King without the passion, the Messiah without the Cross, the Savior without the suffering. But Jesus resisted the devil's deceits, He saw through his lies, He repelled his charms. He had come to die, and die He would. For there is no other way for creation to be renewed but by the death of God's Son upon the Tree of the Cross.

People sometimes think that Jesus' temptations were nothing, since He is the divine Son of God. They consider His sufferings as empty gestures, devoid of true pathos and pain, since He is God's divine Word, the One by whom all things were made. If Jesus of Nazareth is really God's Son in human flesh, they say, what can it mean that He is tempted and suffers? Isn't it a joke? And a bad one at that! And if His sufferings consisted in but half a day on a cross, do not thousands and even millions of people suffer much more than He? How many people there must be who would gladly hang on a cross for a few hours in order to free themselves of months, years, and even decades of the most agonizing suffering and pain! And to be raised up for everlasting life but a day and a half later—who wouldn't wish it? And who wouldn't endure it?

The truth is, however, that Jesus' temptations and sufferings, precisely because He is God's eternal Son in real human flesh, are incomparably more terrifying and agonizing than those of any "mere man," and of all "mere men" who ever were or will be. For Jesus is *God,* experiencing *as God* in His own human soul and body the rejections of His creatures, the betrayals of His brothers, and the abandonment of His own God and Father on the Cross, for the sake of reconciling all creation with Himself in perfect, unending communion and life. In this sense it is wholly accurate to say that no creaturely mind, of men or of angels, can even begin to imagine the magnitude of the temptations and sufferings of Jesus Christ for the sake of His beloved world. In Him all temptations and all sufferings that ever were or will be are experienced to the boundless infinity of His divine person. His, therefore, are temptations and sufferings which transcend creaturely comprehension. They literally cannot be fathomed.

They can hardly even be imagined. They can only be wondered at with speechless adoration and wordless praise: His silence in death can only be met by our silence in awe-inspired amazement!

> Since therefore the children share in flesh and blood, He Himself likewise partook of the same nature, that through death He might destroy him who has the power of death, that is, the devil, and deliver all those who through fear of death were subject to lifelong bondage. For surely it is not with angels that He is concerned but with the descendants of Abraham. Therefore He had to be made like His brethren in every respect, so that He might become a merciful and faithful high priest in the service of God, to make expiation for the sins of the people. For because He Himself has suffered and been tempted, He is able to help those who are tempted. (Heb. 2:14 18)

This is the mystery of mysteries. It forms the very life of the lenten spring. It is the mystery that lies at the heart of life itself.

> When creation saw You naked on the Cross,
> its Maker and Creator,
> it lamented and was transfixed with fear:
> The sun hid its rays;
> the earth trembled;
> the rocks were split;
> the temple's light was darkened;
> the dead were raised from the tombs.
> The angelic powers cried in amazement:
> "O wonder! The Judge of all is judged!
> He voluntarily suffers for the renewal of the world,
> its salvation!"[1]

---

[1]Fourth Tuesday vespers.

37

Let Him Take Up His Cross
and Follow Me

It is not enough for Christians to believe in the crucifixion and resurrection of Jesus. It is not enough for us to "preach Christ crucified" (1 Cor. 1:23). It is not enough for us to bow down before the Cross, and to decorate and venerate and kiss it at church services. Christians must take up the Cross in their own lives. We must be co-crucified with Christ in order to share His glory, and to experience, even in this world, the beauty and power, the peace and joy of the Kingdom of God.

> And He called to Him the multitude with His disciples, and said to them, "If any man would come after Me, let him deny himself and take up his cross and follow Me. For whoever would save his life will lose it; and whoever loses his life for My sake and the gospel's will save it. For what does it profit a man, to gain the whole world and forfeit his life? For what can a man give in return for his life? For whoever is ashamed of Me and of My words in this adulterous and sinful generation, of him will the Son of man also be ashamed, when He comes in the glory of His Father with the holy angels." And He said to them, "Truly, I say to you, there are some standing here who will not taste death before they see the kingdom of God come with power." (Mk. 8:34-9:1)[1]

[1]This is the gospel reading for the divine liturgy of the Third Sunday of Lent, the Veneration of the Cross.

St. Innocent of Alaska, the great missionary who died in the end of the last century as the Metropolitan of Moscow, describes what it means for a person to take up his Cross. These are his words from his little missionary book on the Christian life called *The Way to the Kingdom of Heaven.*[2]

Jesus said: "Whoever wishes to follow Me, let him deny himself, take up his cross and follow Me." The first duty . . . is to *deny oneself.* To deny oneself means to give up one's bad habits; to root out of the heart all that ties us to the world; not to cherish bad thoughts and desires; to suppress every evil thought; to avoid occasions of sin; not to desire or to do anything out of self-love, but to do everything out of love for God. To deny oneself, according to St. Paul means *to be dead to sin . . . but alive to God.*

A Christian's second duty is to *take up his cross.* The word *cross* means sufferings, sorrows and adversities. To take up one's cross means to bear without grumbling everything unpleasant, painful, sad, difficult and oppressive that may happen to us in life.

Thus whether anyone offends you, or laughs at you, or causes you grief, sorrow or annoyance; or you have done good to someone and instead of thanking you, he rises up against you and even makes trouble; or you want to do good, but you are not given the chance; or some misfortune has happened such as sickness; or with all your activity and untiring labors you are suffering from want and poverty and are so hard pressed that you cannot make ends meet; or besides that you are in some personal difficulty—bear all this without malice, without grumbling, without criticism, without complaint, that is, without regarding yourself as offended and without expecting any earthly reward in return,

[2]The full title of this book by John Veniaminov, the Alaskan missionary who became Bishop Innocent and finally the Metropolitan of Moscow, is *The Indication of the Way to the Kingdom of Heaven.* It was published some years ago in Indiana, Pennsylvania, and is now out of print in English. See *Saint Innocent, Apostle to America* by Paul D. Garrett.

but bear it all with love, with joy and with courageous
strength.

. . . [S]o far we have spoken of exterior crosses, but
there are interior crosses as well. . . .

Interior crosses can be found at all times, and more
easily than exterior ones. You have only to direct your
attention to yourself and examine yourself with a sense
of repentance, and a thousand interior crosses will at
once present themselves to you. . . .

We can never see the condition of our inner self in
all of its nakedness or vividly realize its dangers without special grace and help from God, because the interior of our soul is always hidden from us by our
self-love, prejudices, passions, worldly cares, delusions.
And if it sometimes happens to us that we see the
condition of our inner selves, we only see it super-
ficially and no more than our reason and conscience
can show us.

But when the Lord is pleased to reveal to us the
state of our souls, then we . . . feel sharply that our
hearts are corrupt and perverted, our souls are defiled
and we are merely the slaves of sin and passions
which have mastered us and do not allow us to draw
near to God. We see that even our supposed good
deeds are all mixed with sin and are not the fruit of
true love, but are the products of various passions and
circumstances . . . and then we most certainly suffer!
. . . Now you see what interior crosses are! For some
these crosses are . . . oppressive . . . prolonged. It all
depends on the particular person . . . [but] whoever
wants to be cured will bear anything in order to be
freed.

Interior crosses are sometimes so burdensome that
the sufferer can find no consolation whatever in anything.

All this can happen to you too! But in whatever
position you may be, and whatever sufferings of the
soul you may feel, do not despair and do not think that
the Lord has abandoned you. NO! God will always

be with you and will invisibly strengthen you even when it seems to you that you are on the very brink of perdition.

God will never allow you to be tried and tempted more than He sees fit. Do not despair and do not be afraid. With full submission surrender totally to Him. Have patience and pray. He is always our Loving Father. Even if He permits a person who has surrendered to Him to fall into temptation, it is only in order to make him realize more clearly his own impotence, weakness and nothingness ... to teach him never to trust in himself and to show that no one can do anything good without God. And if the Lord leads a person into suffering and lays crosses upon him, it is only to heal his soul, to make him like Jesus Christ, and perfectly to purify his heart in which He Himself wishes to dwell with His Son and the Holy Spirit.

The Cross of Christ is the "law of Lent." It is the "tree of life" which blossoms in the lenten spring with the fruits of the Holy Spirit.

The Cross of the Lord is ever adored
as the binding of pleasures, the law of Lent!
Those who ceaselessly contemplate the Crucified One
crucify the flesh with its passions and lusts.
Let us also flee from these through a pure fast.
Let us join Him who joined in the passion
because of His love for man,
who has freed our nature from passions,
who possesses great mercy.[3]

You have accounted us worthy
to behold and embrace Your holy Cross with joy.
We beg You now, O God our Savior,
enable us also to attain Your most pure sufferings
by being strengthened through the Fast,

[3]Cheesefare Thursday vespers.

so that we may bow down and sing of Your crucifixion,
by which You have snatched us from death,
returning us to the joyous life of Paradise.
We thankfully glorify You, O Lover of man.[4]

The Church is revealed as a second Paradise,
possessing the Tree of Life as the first Paradise of old.
By touching the Cross, O Lord,
we share Your immortality![5]

[4]Fourth Thursday vespers.
[5]Third Sunday matins.

38

Without Temptations No One Can Be Saved

As long as we are in this world we will be tempted. And we will suffer. There is no avoiding it. We believe that the Son of God came to be tempted and to suffer with us, to help us in our trials and pains. But we ourselves must be tempted. And we must endure. Those who endure to the end are saved (Mt. 24:13).

It is written in the sayings of the fathers that St. Anthony said to St. Poemen: "This is the great work of a man: always to take the blame for his own sins before God and to expect temptation to his last breath."[1] And St. Anthony is also recorded as saying: "Whoever has not experienced temptation cannot enter into the Kingdom of heaven," adding the words often quoted in the Christian spiritual tradition, "without temptations no one can be saved."[2]

Without temptation, no salvation! This is the experience of all of the saints. It was true of Jesus who, being God's own Son, was made perfect through His temptations and sufferings (Heb. 2:10; 5:8-9). And it is true for everyone who is obedient to God the Father in imitation of Christ. There is no other way. God Himself sees to it, the devil, the flesh and wicked people obliging. St. Isaac of Syria writes about it in detail.

As often as you find your way to be peaceful, without variations, be suspicious. For you are deviating from

---

[1]*The Sayings of the Desert Fathers,* St. Anthony, 4.
[2]Ibid., St. Anthony, 5.

the divine ways trodden by the weary footsteps of the saints. The more you proceed on the way towards the city of the kingdom and approach its neighborhood, this will be the sign: you will meet hard temptations. And the nearer you approach, the more difficulties you will find. The hard temptations into which God brings the soul are in accordance with the greatness of His gifts. If there is a weak soul which is not able to bear a very hard temptation and God deals meekly with it, then know that it is not capable of bearing a hard temptation and so is not worthy either of a great gift.

God never gives a large gift and small temptations. So temptations are to be classed in accordance with gifts. Thus from the hardships you are called to endure you may understand the measure of the greatness which your soul has reached. And your comfort will be in proportion to your endurance.

In accordance with your humility you will be given endurance in your distress. And in accordance with your endurance its weight will be lifted from your soul and you will be comforted in your troubles. And in accordance with your comfort, your love of God will increase. And in accordance with your love, your spiritual joy will increase.

When our compassionate Father is of the will to relieve those who are real children in their temptations, He does not take their temptations away from them, but He imparts to them endurance under temptations, and all that good which they receive through it, to the perfection of their souls. May Christ in His grace make us worthy of bearing evils for the sake of His love, with thanksgivings in the heart. Amen.[3]

There is nothing here which is not in the gospels and the scriptures of the apostles. Jesus Himself promised: "In the world you have tribulation; but be of good cheer, I have overcome the world" (Jn. 16:33). And the apostle Paul provides

[3]St. Isaac of Syria, *Helpful Advice Based on Love.*

inspiration for St. Isaac when he writes to the Romans that "we rejoice in our sufferings, knowing that suffering produces endurance, and endurance produces character, and character produces hope, and hope does not disappoint us, because God's love has been poured into our hearts through the Holy Spirit who has been given to us" (Rom. 5:3-5).[4] The lenten spring is the time for the acquisition of the Holy Spirit, with all of the graces and gifts which come to us from God our Father through His Son Jesus. We receive them only if we suffer through our temptations and endure to the end.

> Therefore, since we are surrounded by so great a cloud of witnesses, let us also lay aside every weight, and sin which clings so closely, and let us run with perseverance the race that is set before us, looking to Jesus the pioneer and perfecter of our faith, who for the joy that was set before Him endured the cross, despising the shame, and is seated at the right hand of the throne of God. (Heb. 12:1-2)[5]

---

[4] See also Jas. 1:2-4; 2 Cor. 4:7-12, 6:4-10.
[5] The end of the epistle reading for the First Sunday of Lent, the feast of the Triumph of Orthodoxy.

39

Partaking of Christ's Body

For those poor members of the Orthodox Church who still partake of Christ's body and blood only during the Church's lenten seasons and particularly during Great Lent, we have the words of St. John Chrysostom.[1] They are words which even the most frequent partakers of Holy Communion must hear for their salvation.

> If you are the Body of Christ, bear the Cross, for He bore it. Bear spitting, bear beating, bear nails. Such was that Body. . . . Our discourse is concerning this Body, and as many of us as partake of that Body and taste of that Blood are partaking of that which is in no way different from that Body, nor separate from it.
>
> Consider that we taste of that Body which sits above, which is adored by angels, which is next to that Power which is incorruptible. How many ways of salvation are open to us! He has made us to be His own Body! And He has given to us His own Body! And yet not one of these things turns us away from what is evil. O the darkness, the depth of the abyss, the apathy! After all this some still set their affections on money, and some on carnal pleasures and others are carried captive by their passions!
>
> I observe many partaking of Christ's Body lightly

[1]The lenten seasons of the Church are the fast before Easter, the forty-day advent season before Christmas, the fifteen days before the Dormition of the Virgin Mary (August 15), and the period between the first Sunday

and just as it happens, rather from custom and form than consideration and understanding. When, some say, the holy season of lent sets in, whatever a man may be, he partakes of the mysteries. . . . And yet it is not lent that makes a fit time for approaching, but it is sincerity and purity of soul. With this, approach at all times! Without it, never!

Consider them who partook of the sacrifices in the Old Testament. . . . They were always purifying themselves. And do you, when you draw near to the Sacrifice at which the very angels tremble, do you measure the matter by the season of the year? And how will you present yourself before the judgment seat of Christ who presume upon His Body with polluted hands and lips? You would not presume to kiss a king with an unclean mouth, and do you kiss the King of Heaven with an unclean soul? It is an outrage!

Observe the vast inconsistency of the thing. At other times of the year you do not come to communion; no, not even though you often may be clean. But when Easter comes, however flagrant an act you may have committed, you come. O, the force of custom and prejudice! In vain the daily Sacrifice! In vain do we stand at the altar! There is no one to partake!

These things I am saying not to induce you to partake in any manner, but that you should render yourself worthy to partake in a proper manner. Are you not worthy of the Sacrifice, nor of communion? If not, then you are not worthy either of the prayers.

Look, I beg you. A royal table is set before you. Angels serve at the table. The King Himself is there. And do you stand gaping? Are your garments defiled, and yet you take no account of it? Or are they clean? Then fall down and partake!

Tell me, suppose someone were invited to a feast, and were to wash his hands, and sit down, and be all

after Pentecost and the feast of Sts. Peter and Paul (June 29). Until this century, in both East and West, these were the periods for the lay people to partake of Holy Communion.

ready at the table, and after all this, refuse to partake?
Is he not insulting the man who invited him? Were it
not better for such a person never to have come at all?
Now it is in just this same way that you have come
here. You have sung the hymn [Holy! Holy! Holy!].
You have declared yourself to be in the number of
the worthy by not departing with them that are unworthy [i.e., the uninitiated and the defiled].[2] Why
stay, and not partake of the table? I am unworthy, you
will say. Then you are also unworthy of that communion which you have had in the prayers. For it is
not by means of the offerings only, but also by the
songs that the Holy Spirit descends all around.

You are no more allowed to be here than the
catechumen is. For it is not at all the same thing never
to have reached the mysteries, than when you have
reached them, to stumble at them and despise them,
and to make yourself unworthy of this thing.

One might venture to mention more points which
are yet more terrifying. Not to burden your understanding, however, let these be enough. They who are
not brought to their right senses by these, certainly
will not be with more.

That I may not then be the means of increasing
your condemnation, I beg you, not to forbear coming,
but to render yourself worthy both of being present
and of approaching.

He has invited us to heaven, to the table of the
great and wonderful King, and do we shrink and hesi-
tate, instead of hastening and running to it? And what
then is our hope of salvation? We cannot lay the blame
on our weakness. We cannot blame our nature. It is

[2]In times past those who were not yet baptized (i.e., the uninitiated),
and those who had sinned and were under penance (i.e., the defiled), had
physically to leave the church before the offering of the bread and wine at
the Eucharist. The command for such persons to depart is still part of the
Orthodox eucharistic service. The exclamation "The doors! The doors!"
before the recitation of the creed at the divine liturgy indicates that the
doors to the church building are to be closed to all who are not competent
to offer and receive Holy Communion.

indolence and nothing else that renders us unworthy!

Come together here, not in vain and not by chance, but with fear and reverence. For you shall behold with boldness Christ Himself in heaven, and shall be counted worthy of that heavenly kingdom which, may God grant we may all attain, in Jesus Christ our Lord, with whom, with the Father, together with the Holy Spirit, be glory, power, and honor now and ever, and unto ages of ages. Amen.[3]

---

[3]*On Ephesians,* homily 3. See also *On Timothy,* homily 5.

40

Going Up to Jerusalem

On the last Sunday of Great Lent, the gospel reading at the Eucharist tells of Jesus and His disciples going up to Jerusalem.[1]

> And they were on the road, going up to Jerusalem, and Jesus was walking ahead of them; and they were amazed, and those who followed were afraid. And taking the twelve again, He began to tell them what was to happen to Him, saying, "Behold, we are going up to Jerusalem; and the Son of man will be delivered to the chief priests and the scribes, and they will condemn Him to death, and deliver Him to the Gentiles; and they will mock Him, and spit upon Him, and scourge Him, and kill Him; and after three days He will rise." (Mk. 10:32-34)

The first time that Jesus told the apostles that He was to suffer and die was immediately after Peter confessed Him for the first time to be the Christ, the Son of the living God. Jesus then announced that the Messiah was the Suffering Servant, the One rejected and crucified in order to be raised and glorified by the Father. When Peter rebelled at this revelation, the Lord rebuked him with harsh words, even calling him Satan. Then, in the course of the festival of booths, Jesus took Peter, James and John to the mountain and was transfigured before them in glory, speaking with

[1] The forty days of Lent finish on the eve of Lazarus Saturday. Formally speaking, Lazarus Saturday, Palm Sunday and Holy Week are not part of Great Lent.

Moses and Elijah about the "exodus" that He was to make in Jerusalem.[2] Coming down from the mountain, He spoke again about His impending betrayal, suffering, death and resurrection on the third day.[3]

When the disciples were going up to Jerusalem with Jesus, it is recorded that they were amazed and afraid. Their amazement, no doubt, was from the strange and marvelous character of what was happening. Their fear was certainly from Jesus' predictions about His fate, soon to be fulfilled, for they knew that the Lord's enemies were really seeking to kill Him. As they went their way, they continued to ask about their place in the kingdom. And their amazement and fear must have been more greatly magnified at the Master's response:

> But Jesus said to them, "You do not know what you are asking. Are you able to drink the cup that I drink, or to be baptized with the baptism with which I am baptized?" And they said to Him, "We are able." And Jesus said to them, "The cup that I drink you will drink; and with the baptism with which I am baptized, you will be baptized; but to sit at My right hand or at My left is not Mine to grant, but it is for those for whom it has been prepared." And when the ten heard it, they began to be indignant at James and John. And Jesus called them to Him and said to them, "You know that those who are supposed to rule over the Gentiles lord it over them, and their great men exercise authority over them. But it shall not be so among you; but whoever would be great among you must be your servant, and whoever would be first among you must be slave of all. For the Son of man also came not to be served but to serve, and to give His life as a ransom for many." (Mk. 10:38-45)

[2]See Lk. 9:31. The word "exodus" is translated here literally. It refers to the original passover/exodus of Israel which is the type of Christ's pascha in Jerusalem. The RSV translates this word as "departure." The KJV says "decease."

[3]See Mt. 16-17, Mk. 8-9, Lk. 9.

Whatever happens during the forty days of Great Lent, whether we think, according to our limited understanding, that we have done well, or whether we learn once more the bitter but most blessed lesson of our incapacity to accomplish even the smallest of our good intentions, the result—if we are yet the least bit alive—will be the same every year: we go up to Jerusalem with Jesus, like His very first disciples, amazed and afraid! We are filled with wonder and awe at what the Lord brings to pass for the sake of our salvation. If this be so (and may the Lord grant it!), the lenten spring will not have shone forth upon us in vain.

> Make us worthy, O Lover of Man,
> to behold the week of Your Passion,
> for we have finished the forty days of the fast.
> May we glorify Your mighty acts,
> Your unspeakable plan of salvation for our sake.
> O Lord, glory to You![4]

> We have completed the forty days which profit our souls.
> Now let us beg of the Lover of man:
> "Enable us to see the Holy Week of Your Passion,
> that we may glorify Your mighty work,
> Your wonderful plan of salvation for us,
> singing with one heart and one voice:
> 'O Lord, glory to You!' "[5]

[4]Sixth Friday matins.
[5]Sixth Friday vespers.

Select Bibliography

Books here referred to, and others recommended for lenten reading.

Bishop Alexander. *Father John of Kronstadt: A Life.* Crestwood, NY: St. Vladimir's Seminary Press, 1979.

Brianchaninov, Bishop Ignatius. *The Arena: An Offering to Contemporary Monasticism.* Madras, India: The Diocesan Press, 1970.

Cassian, St. John. *Teachings on the Spiritual Life.* Willits, CA: Eastern Orthodox Books, n.d.

Igumen Chariton, compiler. *The Art of Prayer: An Orthodox Anthology.* Translated by E. Kadloubovsky and E. M. Palmer. London: Faber & Faber, 1966.

Climacus, St. John. *The Ladder of Divine Ascent.* Translated by Colm Luibheid and Norman Russell. New York: Paulist Press, 1982.

Elchaninov, Fr. Alexander. *The Diary of a Russian Priest.* Translated by Helen Iswolsky. Crestwood, NY: St. Vladimir's Seminary Press, 1982.

Fedotov, George P., editor and compiler. *A Treasury of Russian Spirituality.* Belmont, MA: Nordland, 1975.

Garrett, Paul D. *St. Innocent, Apostle to America.* Crestwood, NY: St. Vladimir's Seminary Press, 1979.

The Lenten Triodion. Translated by Mother Mary and Archimandrite Kallistos Ware. London: Faber & Faber, 1978.

Life of our Holy Father Seraphim of Sarov and Akathist. Jordanville, NY: Holy Trinity Monastery, 1967.

Starets Macarius of Optino. *Russian Letters of Direction: 1834-1860.* Selected and translated by Iulia de Beausobre. Crestwood, NY: St. Vladimir's Seminary Press, 1975.

St. Nicodemus of the Holy Mountain, editor. *Unseen Warfare.* Revised by Bishop Theophan the Recluse. Translated by E. Kadloubovsky and G.E.H. Palmer. Crestwood, NY: St. Vladimir's Seminary Press, 1978.

St. Nikodimos of the Holy Mountain and St. Makarios of Corinth, compilers. *The Philokalia,* vol. 1. Translated and edited by G. E. H. Palmer, Philip Sherrard, and Kallistos Ware. London: Faber & Faber, 1979.

The Sayings of the Desert Fathers: The Alphabetical Collection. Translated by Benedicta Ward, S.L.G. London: Mowbray & Co.; USA: Cistercian Publications, 1975.

Schmemann, Fr. Alexander. *Great Lent.* Crestwood, NY: St. Vladimir's Seminary Press, 1974.

Sergieff, Fr. John Ilyitch. *My Life in Christ: Extracts from the Diary of Father John of Kronstadt.* Translated by E. E. Goulaeff. London: Cassell & Co., 1897; reprinted, Jordanville, NY: Holy Trinity Monastery, 1971.

Archimandrite Sophrony. *Wisdom from Mount Athos: The Writings of Staretz Silouan, 1866-1938.* Translated by Rosemary Edmonds. Crestwood, NY: St. Vladimir's Seminary Press, 1974.

The Way of a Pilgrim and *The Pilgrim Continues His Way.* Translated by R. M. French. New York: Seabury Press, a Crossroad Book, 1965.

Zander, Valentine. *St. Seraphim of Sarov.* Translated by Sister Gabriel Anne, S.S.C. Crestwood, NY, 1975.